MIRACLES
MADE POSSIBLE

MIRACLES
MADE POSSIBLE

AN AUTOBIOGRAPHICAL DISCOVERY OF GOD

WILLIAM THOMAS TUCKER

HAMPTON ROADS
PUBLISHING COMPANY, INC.

Cover design by Marjoram Productions
Cover photograph copyright © 2004 Jonathan Friedman
"The Paradoxical Commandments" are reprinted by permission
of Kent M. Keith. © Copyright Kent M. Keith 1968, renewed 2001.

Hampton Roads Publishing Company, Inc.
1125 Stoney Ridge Road
Charlottesville, VA 22902

434-296-2772
fax: 434-296-5096
e-mail: hrpc@hrpub.com
www.hrpub.com

If you are unable to order this book from your local
bookseller, you may order directly from the publisher.
Call 1-800-766-8009, toll-free.

Library of Congress Cataloging-in-Publication Data

Tucker, William Thomas.
  Miracles made possible : an autobiographical discovery of God / William
Thomas Tucker.
     p. cm.
  ISBN 1-57174-389-8 (alk. paper)
  1. Tucker, William Thomas. 2. Spiritual biography--United States. 3.
Miracles. I. Title.
  BL73.T83A3 2004
  204'.092--dc22

                                    2004004396

                        ISBN 1-57174-389-8

                        10 9 8 7 6 5 4 3 2 1

            Printed on acid-free paper in the United States

To

Pamela and Carter,

Penelope and Paul,

Matthew and Little Lauren

Contents

Preface

This book is dedicated to all of the self-identified atheists and agnostics who, while either denying the existence of God or claiming not to know one way or another, are sometimes more in league with God than they realize. Sometimes they are more in league with God and God's wishes than those who profess faith. I have been there, but was awakened by a series of otherwise unexplainable events that proved the existence and love of the great "I Am" to me. My story within these pages recounts that journey and the revealing of God to me, so that you, too, may experience an understanding of God. The ultimate result, hopefully, will be that the proofs and lessons learned will spur you on your own journey back to the bosom of God from whence we all came. Further, I hope that you will come to realize that you, too, can have any miracle you desire from God—on demand.

Of course, believers as well are invited to come closer to God through sharing the experiences in this book.

The purpose of this book is to relate a series of my life experiences that proved to me, beyond a doubt, the *existence* of God and God's proactive role in our everyday lives. I hope that by so sharing these personal events, you the reader will come to a new, or renewed, belief in God to enrich your life.

God exists! Of that, I no longer have any doubt. Those who doubt have only to reach out to God and ask God to reveal God's Self in their lives: Ask, and you shall receive. However, as it will become painfully clear, this is the most difficult thing for any man, woman, or child to do, although it is far less difficult for a child. It is difficult because it ignites or triggers a fundamental fear in us. The "fear" is that if it turns out that there is no God, then we are truly alone. The fear of that is almost dev-astating. Better to not know than to be disappointed.

Within these pages, you will read of multiple examples of God proac-tively blessing God's children—us—with God's beneficence through real-life miracles. A miracle, in the true sense of the word, means a hap-penstance that can be explained no other way. Our first understanding of a miracle is that it is a great big windfall. An unexplainable healing of the physical body is one example, or the receipt of millions of dollars simply for the asking, or any myriad of wonderful events, both large and small, and in between.

I ask not for your faith. To begin, I ask you to accept nothing I say without question. Please, be skeptical. Challenge any theory or state-ment; anything and everything is open to your scrutiny. For only you can decide what you believe concerning God's existence or non-existence. I will show how I have come to see the proofs of God's existence all around us. Whether you choose to look at them, analyze them for what they are and come to grips with them, or turn away, is your business. However, if you have not seen this evidence in the past, the problem may be you have not known where or how to look. Maybe the answer for you lies within. . . .

An analogy is, perhaps, appropriate here. To me, God is like elec-tricity. It's always there, all around you, in the walls of your home, wait-ing silently to serve. You can't see it. You can't taste it, nor hear it. If someone unfamiliar with electricity were to enter your home, you would have trouble explaining the concept of electricity, and much trouble proving that it existed in your walls, unseen and unfelt as it is. The only way you could *prove* to your visitor that it is there would be to demon-strate its effects. You could plug a lamp into the wall and turn it on. The light blazing forth would amaze your visitor, would it not? One still would not understand electricity, but the effect of light would prove that some unseen and powerful energy is there at work. One could no longer doubt its existence.

I think God is like that. I have come to realize that God is here, there, everywhere, waiting to serve you and me. We busy ourselves every day with earthly concerns. We go to work, interact with our fam-ilies or friends, shop, pay bills, drive places, perform our jobs, and run our businesses. That's why we call it "busy-ness." We stay busy. But have you ever considered what God's job is? What God's busy-ness is?

What does God do all day? You have heard the answer many times through many languages, religions, books, and cultures. That answer has never changed. God is busy performing miracles, upon request or *expectation,* for billions of people all over the planet every day. We won't see them, though, if we don't ask for them, *believe* in them, look for them, acknowledge them, or accredit them.

It is in the *expectation* that unbelievers also get miracles from God. I understand that they don't credit God with the happy result of their "luck," but God isn't necessarily looking for credit lines. God has made mankind a promise, and God *always* lives up to God's promises. God promises that God will answer *all* prayers that are *first believed in* . . . and the answer is *never* "No."

I recognize that even a very faithful person may sometimes make a request of God and not have it fulfilled. Despite the miraculous events that I relate in this book, that happens to me regularly. When that happens, we are perplexed. "How could this be?" we ask ourselves. The obvious answer—God does not exist and is only a figment of mankind's collective imagination—is too horrible even to consider. So there must be a better explanation as to why God has let us down.

Many representatives of faiths, when pressed for an answer, make up a logical answer. Some declare, "That is the supernatural mystery"; others announce "The mind of man is too feeble to be able to understand the mind of God"; still others rationalize, "God *does* answer all prayers, but sometimes the answer is 'No.'"

Is that possible? Is that written down anywhere? In any of the world's religious books? Has anybody on the planet gotten a quote from God wherein God says, "I will answer all prayers. But, sometimes My answer will be 'No'"? If the answer *could* be "No," is that an acceptable response to "God answers all prayers"? Isn't a denial the same as no answer? If my child asks me for candy, and I turn my back on him and do not respond, have I "answered" his request by giving him what he wants? Or have I denied him by ignoring his request? Thereby, by definition, I am *not* answering his request.

Consider this: You probably feel that man is fallible and that God is infallible. After all, all religions preach that. So, I'll concede that point for the moment. If there is a breakdown in communication between man and God, whose "fault" do you think it is? The Infallible One? Or fallible mankind's? My money's on you and me.

Maybe it isn't God who drops the ball. Maybe it's you and me. Maybe God understands our communication (request for a miracle) very well, but you and I fail to accurately communicate our heart's desires, fearlessly, wholeheartedly, faithfully. Could that be the case? Of course, if you are an atheist, you probably think you are not even asking. Why bother, nobody's listening anyway. That is, until your back is to the wall and you desperately need help, a miracle. Then you may reach out, even if you don't believe, or don't *think* you believe.

It has been said that there are no atheists in a foxhole. Soldiers in a foxhole (scared to death of dying in battle) always turn to God in their hour of need, whether they are faithful or atheist. Faced with life or death, I've never met anybody who voluntarily opts for death, and that includes suicides. Suicidal people view death as an acceptable alternative to what they perceive is even worse, the pain they are experiencing. What is that pain? The pain of self-rejection. Self-rejection is the ultimate denial of God. I'll explore that later in this book.

So let's turn to the first chapter and take a journey of discovery as I recount events I could never have imagined happening. It's all true and verifiable, and it may open your eyes, your mind, and, most importantly, your heart. You are about to come home, home to the you that *is* you, home to your embryonic beginnings of life on this planet, back to remembering Who You Are, and What You Are, and you will rejoice.

This book recounts the discovery of the irrefutable existence of God by a former atheist. I am an ordinary man, living an ordinary life. Even when God stepped into my life during the most Job-like trying times and delivered miracles to me, miracles are so commonplace in everybody's life, that fact alone does not make this book spectacular.

What the reader will discover, as we travel the road I experienced, as I recount my life's experiences, is that I had so many unexplainable events occur in my life as to awaken me to *the process* by which miracles are attained. My experiences led me to a deeper level of understanding than most people reach.

I explore the depths of that understanding and reveal the irrefutable secrets of life that, although in conflict with science and conventional religions of all faiths, are nonetheless known to all of mankind by virtue of the fact that God has put the truth of miracles in all the hearts of all mankind.

Many people, perhaps billions, experience at least one miracle in their lifetimes. They may choose to call it "luck." Or, they may burn candles in thanks. But they more often than not do not know why they were blessed with this particular miracle at this particular time. I have come to realize that we—each of us—are at the "cause" of the miracle we get. And, therefore, we can each have as many miracles as we desire . . . simply for the *asking* and *believing!* This book reveals the concept behind getting miracles, so that the reader may invoke this power whenever they feel the need. Journey with me, then, as I relate the story of my life and the miraculous events that led me back to God.

Acknowledgment

I wish to acknowledge my good friend Neale Donald Walsch. I don't know if I have the right to call him "my good friend" because I have never asked him. However, whether he would agree to be called my friend or not, he has become my good and faithful friend because of the message of God's love that he has brought into my life through his books. I loved his books because they substantiated everything about God that I had surmised for myself over my lifetime of experiences. Neale and I have grappled with the same issues of organized religion, from different perspectives. Neale as an "insider" (being Catholic), and I as a religious "outsider" who couldn't find a religion that wanted to abide my "individuality."

There are three distinctions between Neale and me that I would like to point out. First of all, God has communicated the same information to me as he has to Neale, but God doesn't talk to me verbally. He communicates by bringing miracles into my life, literally demonstrating His love.

Second, Neale has written his books from a "New Bible" point of view, putting God's message in the traditional Old and New Testaments in proper perspective. I, on the other hand, frequently quote or draw us back to the original, traditional Bible (as we have in today's translations) and relate Walsch's "new" message to the original words. I do this because the original words are true. Mankind has just twisted them to suit its own interpretations. I am in awe that mankind has not altered the actual words in the Bible to suit our theories and perceptions over the millennia. God must have had a hand in that! For example, Jesus said, if smitten on one cheek, offer your other . . . while the Crusaders charged into battle calling to kill in the name of Christ. I don't understand why they never bothered to change Jesus' words in their Bible to, "Go kill in my name." That would have justified their actions. But they didn't. They left Christ intact, and their actions were opposite of the admonition from Christ.

Third, Neale vacillates between referring to God in the male gender and female gender, and even says in *Friendship With God* that maybe He's neither. I'd like to clarify this particular point. It amazes me how so many people profess to believe in the Bible without ever having read it, much less understanding what it says. To begin with, they think it's a book—but it's not. It's very name from the Latin *biblia* means "many books," and indeed, each "section" in it is so labeled—Genesis, the First Book of Moses; Exodus, the Second Book of Moses, etc.

Furthermore, most people do not even realize that the Bible they are familiar with is not even close to being the whole Bible. Over the centuries, various ecumenical councils and even the publishers have met and decided which books to put in and which to leave out. They also decide which translation to use from the often ambiguous original Greek or Latin or Hebrew texts. Frequently—every 20 years or so for the past 2,000 years—they change the very words, sometimes dramatically! For example, The Book of Thomas was unearthed from the Dead Sea caves in 1947 and has not been touched in these 2,000 years. Christ's words, as reported by the disciple Thomas are radically rougher than the words we have in the other four Gospels. Our present-day Gospels have been "smoothed out" to make Christ appear more "learned."

For centuries we have been referring to God as "Him," as a male. Why? Because, our English translation comes from the original Greek texts. There are three genders in Greek (and in the earlier Hebrew texts)—male, female, and neuter, or "it." God, whose pronoun was "It" literally translates as "Godhead," neither male nor female. In 1378 A.D., John Wycliff made the first translation of the Bible to English, and when he came to "Godhead" he was stumped. He had to pick one of the only two genders in English to be God's pronoun. Now, John was a male . . . enough said.

Literalists will *tell* you that the Bible says that "God created man in

His own Image." Not so. Read the *entire* sentence. It says, "God made man in His own Image; male and female made He them, in His Image." Now, if we replace the errant translation with the correct (original) words, it comes out, "God made man(kind) in Godhead's own Image; male and female made Godhead them in Godhead's Image." So, God is *not* "male," nor "female," nor "neither." God is All. In my text, I attempt to avoid "Him" or "Her," "He" or "She." I use God or God's to show possession whenever possible. I trust this attention to accuracy will not distract the reader.

Introduction

By Neale Donald Walsch,
author of *Conversations with God, Books 1, 2, 3,*
and other works

I first became acquainted with Bill Tucker when I learned of the wonderful miracles that have occurred in his life. I was immediately taken with how Bill had been putting into practice the messages presented in the *Conversations with God* books about how life and faith works.

I had a chance to meet Bill personally when he attended one of my lectures, and we had the opportunity to discuss some of his experiences. A few months later, as I was compiling true-life stories of miracles for my book *Moments of Grace*, I selected one of Bill's stories from the many hundreds I have received from readers. But Bill has had so many interesting and significantly representative experiences in his life that I asked him if I could include a second story in the book. So there are two Bill Tucker anecdotes in *Moments of Grace*, and that attests to the fact that this man has led a fascinating life in which he has learned to call forth miracles from the universe.

Because he has had so many wonderful experiences, I suggested that Bill write a book of his own and share all of his stories with the world. I'm glad that he has done so, because the telling of his stories makes it clear that such experiences—while exciting and inspiring—need not be considered the province of a select few. We are all miracle workers, and the grace of God and the power of God and the help of God are available to every man and every woman and every child in every moment, and that is the point here.

The grand illusion of our world is that miracles are rare—and that this is, in fact, what qualifies them to be called miracles. Bill Tucker shows here that miracles are normal occurrences when one is thinking accurate thoughts—about oneself and about God. The challenge is to change our belief systems, to change our thoughts.

That's all Bill did. He did it early in his life, and it has served him in many wonderful ways. So read, now, how a regular, ordinary person with normal skills and abilities, just like you and me, experienced some breathtaking, stunning "moments of grace" in his life—and how you can do exactly the same in yours.

—Neale Donald Walsch

1

Children Know about God

In the Beginning . . .

The purpose of this book is to relate my experiences in the discovery of God and the miracles God performs in our lives on a daily basis. Miracles simply for the asking and believing. Hopefully, you will derive some insight on this subject as you travel this road in the book.

Until much later in life, I had no idea where my initial belief in the existence of God came from. All I know is that from the beginning of memory, I knew God. Later I fell away, but in the beginning, as a child, I knew God. I knew there *was* a God, and I knew that God loved me. My parents were divorced when I was three. My mother had to place my baby sister and me in a foster home while she worked to afford to bring us back. She remarried when I was five, and she and my stepfather retrieved my sister and me from the home of "Aunt" Edna. One of their first acts was to buy a small house with a government G.I. loan. This involved my first conscious remembrance of God.

They took me along one day to shop for a kitchen table. This was the late 1940s, and aluminum and Formica were the inexpensive materials of choice. The store was wall-to-wall with aluminum and Formica table and chair sets. There was only one beautiful knotty pine wood kitchen set that caught my mother's eye. It was also the most costly item in the store. So my parents shopped and shopped and shopped, ruminating over this set and that, but always my mother would gravitate back to the beautiful wood set.

Trailing along, I was ignored while discussions were going on about its cost. Bored and curious, I crawled under the table. I looked up and was horrified. The table was not finished underneath. How could this be? My next thought was, "How could God have sent me to Earth before it was finished, before it was perfect?"

I remember that experience as if it were yesterday, probably because I was so shocked. Somehow, I knew that where I had come from was a place of absolute perfection. I was perplexed. I couldn't believe that I was in a place where unfinished tables were acceptable.

I crawled out from under the table to my mother's side. Tugging on her skirt, I wanted to warn her not to buy the set because it was flawed. It was not perfect. It was unfinished on the underside where grown-ups couldn't see. "Momma, Momma," I insisted, but she just brushed me off with a, "Not now, Billy, Mommy is busy talking to this salesman."

But I persisted. When I finally got her attention and told her of my discovery, she, my father, and the salesman burst out laughing and talked down to me as if I couldn't understand the sophistication of the adult world. I was stunned. I can't remember my exact thoughts after that, but the result was that I accepted that if they wanted to be stupid and buy a half-finished table, they only had themselves to thank.

Of course, this event is not about kitchen table sets. It's about my assumed knowledge of the existence of a God, my Father in heaven, and of my existence before being born. None of that seemed important for many, many years. Of course, I assumed there was a God, and God was my (ultimate) Father, and God sent me to Earth to be born and live here. That all went without saying, and that's the point of the story. Long before I was told anything about God, or attended Sunday school or church, I knew there was a God. It was an inherent part of Who I Was.

The Fall . . .

As a child, I was teased by the other kids for being such a big advocate of God. I refused to smoke cigarettes with them, take candy from the store without paying, or to use swear words because I didn't want to offend God. They mocked and laughed at me. I didn't like being different, but I also did not want to offend God. Over time, a swear word here and there would slip out of my mouth, and I would berate myself heartily for it, chastising myself for having cursed. Then came the revelation from the older kids about sex. I couldn't believe it. What a horrible thing to have to do. (Obviously this revelation came a little too early for me, as I warmed up to the idea in time.)

In fact, I became acclimated to planet Earth and began to fit in with the ways of the world. I became more one of the guys, and spent less time worrying about what God thought.

Then it happened. I'll never forget it as long as I live. It was my final comeuppance. I was 13 years old. It was a Saturday, about mid-morning, and I was sitting on the stoop of our rented duplex situated on a busy street where the speed limit was 35 mph. There were a half-dozen six-year-olds playing kick-the-ball next door. The ball missed its intended player and scooted out between the parked cars into the street. Before the word "Stop!" could issue from my throat, one boy rushed after it out into the street, shooting out between the parked cars. I heard the squeal of tires, the sickening thud, and saw the little body fly through the air.

I was off the stoop in a shot and rushed to the curb, as all of the doors of the homes lining the street burst open and parents rushed, horrified, to the curb. In the street was the bloodied body of the child, crumpled, twisted, and unconscious. People were screaming. I stood transfixed, not knowing what to do. Anything seemed to be too late. Then the driver got out of his car. He was about 42 years old and staggering drunk. He careened his way around to the front of his car, and said loudly, "That'll teach you to run out into the street, ya' little bastard!" And, with that, he climbed back into his car and drove off.

I was frozen into inaction. I didn't have the presence of mind to get his license number. I had never seen death before nor an accident. I was, in fact, only now becoming aware of a world outside my neighborhood and school. It was only a few days before that horrific event that I had started to read the news part of the paper instead of the comics. I was troubled about stories of blacks being treated as second-class citizens, not being able to use a white persons' water fountain or sit at a lunch counter. I was haunted by pictures of naked children running and crying with burned bodies amidst the ravages of war in a foreign land. I was hearing stories told by my parents and uncles about their experiences in World War II. The atrocities made me struggle with how mankind could do such terrible things. It was unthinkable, especially if there was an all-loving God.

The ambulance sirens and angry shouts of adults filled the air as I walked away pondering how a loving God could allow this beautiful innocent child to be maimed while that rotten old drunk driver drove away. "What kind of a place am I in, anyway?" I angrily demanded of no one. "Just what kind of a hellhole world is this?"

There on my front lawn I stared up at the sky. "Help me, Father. I'm losing my faith in You. Help me to understand this." Then it occurred to me: Maybe there isn't an all-loving God. Maybe God is a figment of our imagination, sort of a whistle in the dark against the things we can't understand or control, a buffer against the wild beasts at the cave door. "Oh my god," I thought, at the revelation, "Maybe I am *alone*. Maybe there isn't a God I can count on. Maybe there isn't an omnipresence hovering over me like a protecting blanket."

I lay down on the lawn and whispered, "God. Help me, please. Help me to keep my faith in you. Give me a sign that you are there. Perform a tiny little miracle, just for me, so that I may believe. Make this one blade of grass I'm looking at bend over. Then I'll know that you're there and I have nothing to fear."

I stared at that little blade an inch in front of my nose. Nothing happened. It didn't budge. "God needs a second chance," I rationalized. "God! Make some rain fall, out of this cloudless blue sky, right on my head. Just a few drops that no one else will see. This is just between You and me. I need my faith strengthened. I'm afraid I'm losing my faith in You. Please, just do this one little thing for me, so that I may believe."

I stood for a long time. No rain fell. "So," I thought to myself, "this is it, the end of innocence. There is no God. There is only me. I cannot count on any help throughout life from anyone. I am going to have to take care of me and mine. Whatever fate befalls me throughout life, will only be due to my own ignorance or mistakes. I have to be strong. I have to take care of myself. If I am to have anything in this world, I am going to have to do it for myself. I will have to study hard and get a good education, and work hard—harder than anybody—on my job, so I can't be fired. I'm going to have to work and work and work to be able to afford a house and furniture and clothes for my children, 'cause there ain't anybody here but me." The covenant with myself was sealed. It took a few more weeks before I admitted to myself that I was an atheist, but I finally did.

I kept that to myself. I did not trust anyone with this information. It was all there in front of us for anyone who wanted to face the truth. If they chose not to, maybe they weren't ready to face their fears or their responsibilities. Maybe that's why some drank on a Saturday morning. I knew a lot of adults who drowned their "personal devils" in a bottle. I made another covenant.

If I was going to be responsible for myself, I couldn't afford to cloud my brain. I had seen that booze surely did that. I'm not a teetotaler and I have been drunk in my life, but I can count on one hand the number of times. I certainly did *not* get behind the wheel of a car when inebriated. I learned that lesson firsthand. The last thing in the world I ever wanted was to be responsible for hurting another human being. That's how I thought at age 13. The course of my life for the next 29 years was set.

2

Being of the World, without God

Taking Responsibility

I could not have imagined what was in store for me 29 years later. It is so shocking, so unreal, that it has taken me decades to write it down. I was afraid nobody would understand, afraid people would think I was crazy and lock me up. I was afraid to be rejected by all of mankind, a person without a country, without a place in the world. I was afraid I couldn't find the words to help people to understand me. I needn't have feared. I have since told hundreds of people and, while they are in awe, none has *not* believed me. The reason for that will become clear as this story unfolds. But before I leap forward 29 years, let me give an overview of the events of those 29 years.

I was not a good student in high school. I earned either As or Fs, and hardly anything in between. I dropped out of high school two months before graduation when I learned that I would not be graduating with my class. Angrily, I walked out the door of my school and drove straight to an Air Force recruiting office. The next day I was flying to Lackland Air Force Base in Texas, and spent the next four years in Germany getting my act together.

During what free time I had in high school, and then later in the Air Force, I studied history, religion, and the history of religion to understand how the world got in the shape I found it. I attended many churches: Catholic, Baptist, "Holy Rollers," Lutheran, Presbyterian, and other Protestant churches. I even attended a synagogue with Jewish friends for a while. I got an English version of the Koran and read it. Even the Mormons didn't escape my scrutiny as I read *The Book of Moroni*. I was looking for something, trying to find out if any religion got it right. I was functioning solo, on the outside looking in, but I didn't relish being alone.

I was skeptical. I saw a man on television named Oral Roberts. Roberts was a tent revivalist. That meant he traveled from town to town, set up a gigantic tent, and rallied people to hear his sermons. The highlight of the show was when he would call the lame and the infirm forward to his pulpit. He would lay his hands on the person's forehead, and pray out loud, almost screaming to God. Then he would slam his hand against the person's forehead knocking him off his crutches and flat on his back. He had a couple of assistants positioned to catch the person as he fell. "What a fraud!" I thought. "How can he get away with this charlatan stuff? Are all those people in cahoots with him?"

Oral Roberts was a laughingstock to many people and a lot of people thought he was a fraud. I was mystified at the obvious sincerity of the people he "healed." I was sure that, whatever else was going on, they believed. They always got up, threw their crutches away, and walked away on their own. I shook my head and put it out of my mind. After all, God hadn't performed any miracles on this planet for the past 2,000 years, right? (Of course, today you'd have a hard time explaining that to Oral or his son, Richard Roberts, since they have a huge church and a university as a result of their faith in God's miracles.)

I continued my studies throughout my stay in Europe, but I never found what I was looking for. I did become knowledgeable in religious teachings, beliefs, traditions, and rituals. But, honestly, I found most of them—especially the rituals—a foolish waste of time. Don't get me wrong. I found much I liked. I was now a man without a code, free to decide what I would honor and respect, and what I would not. I could be a master criminal or live a saintly life. It didn't matter, because there was no ultimate punishment for an atheist, except death. If you don't believe in God, then there is no hell, Satan, or any otherworldly thing to fear. There is only that permanent sleep from which no one wakes. The party is over. Finito. Done. Gone.

But I needed a code. I liked Jesus, what He had to say, what He did. I liked His philosophy. I decided that was a good code to live by. But, I determined, I would live it as He preached and lived it, not the way it was taught in the churches I had visited. I had no intention of fearing God. That seemed silly. I understood that Christ said, "When your enemy smites you on the one cheek, turn and offer him your other." That made some sort of sense to me. After all, if I hit someone, I should expect to be hit back. But, I didn't see that "Christian" behavior in the actions of anyone around me. I saw anger. I saw arguments. I saw people lost and turning to drink. I saw wars. I saw hurt.

I read about the Crusades and how the Knights Templar slaughtered "heathens" in the Holy Land to reclaim it in the name of Jesus, and wondered how that exemplified turning the other cheek. I read about the Inquisition and wondered how anybody could rationalize killing anybody else in the name of Christ. Honestly, I could never find one passage in any holy book that endorsed killing as a way to faith.

I saw people rationalizing all sorts of behaviors and beliefs that I could not reconcile with the teachings of any faith. Almost all sermons I ever heard in any religious service, and even on Christian radio stations, were judgments and railings, denigrating anyone who didn't believe the way *they* believed. This one's a sinner and going straight to hell, and that one is defiling the religion. Mostly, these types weren't concerned with atheists, although they seemed to hate secular humanists with a passion. Mostly they were attacking people of other faiths or people of their own faith with whom they disagreed. It was all too much condemnation for me. I was glad to be out of the clutches of any religion.

I reconciled my original sin guilt by realizing that I can't be born a sinner because of the act of some guy born thousands of years before me who defied God and ate the fruit of knowledge. I reasoned that if God wanted to offer me the choice of either accepting God with blind faith and living forever, or eating the fruit of the Tree of the Knowledge of Good and Evil, I'd pass on that fruit.

I took it a step further. In the age-old debate between religionists and secular humanists about the origin and creation of mankind (Big Bang theory versus Garden of Eden), I came to realize that they both had to be wrong.

When the English translation of the Bible says Adam and Eve "ate," that word can mean ingest, but it can also mean accept, as in "Adam 'ate' a lie." Then, "fruit" can mean the apple that grows on a tree, or result, as in "Adam's reward was the 'fruit' of his labors." "Tree" can mean a leafy perennial plant, or it can be a "representative relationship structure" as in "the family tree." Therefore, I reasoned, a more correct interpretation of the sentence, "Adam and Eve ate the fruit of knowledge from the tree of life and knew good from evil" might be: "The first man and the first woman accepted the result of the knowledge of good and evil."

I merrily went on my way, turning the other cheek, only I called it "considering the source." Much later, I learned to forgive them, and still later, I learned to love them for their failings. I realized it wasn't me they were striking out against, but rather they were acting out of inner pain and self-rejection that someone had wrongly planted in them.

In fact, according to semantics theory, when people talk about someone or something else, they are not making a statement about that other thing at all. They are describing their own perception of it. All statements are colored by our perceptual experiences, and therefore are statements of how *we see* them, *not* how they truly are. Therefore, when people say that we are too defensive, they are not describing us at all. They are merely describing how they feel about us and how they perceive us. Is that an accurate interpretation of our behavior? Maybe.

Maybe we are being defensive, or maybe they feel threatened by us and can find no other expression to overpower us. What is important to hear when anybody says anything that is a "judgment call" is that we should hear their feelings and seek to understand why they are making that particular judgment. Then, rather than being defensive about that allegation, we might hear what is behind it, and address that.

I finished high school while in the service, and then went on to graduate cum laude from college, got a succession of jobs that fulfilled me and allowed me full and free expression of Who I Wanted To Be—a corporate executive in the world of business, a position that allowed me to be creative and responsible. I joined the Naval Reserve after college because of urgings within me to do something patriotic.

As a teenager I had a gotten the only job I seemed to be qualified for. I sold newspaper subscriptions door-to-door, and over time became a good salesman, developing theories on how to sell. Those skills seemed to be valuable in every job I had after that. I had dreamed of being an advertising man, and did that sort of work for many years.

I married my high school sweetheart, bought a home in the suburbs, and began raising our two daughters. I drove a nice car, was able to set a little money aside, invest some, and eventually we bought a second car. I found much personal satisfaction over the years as a volunteer in community services such as the Boy Scouts and Junior Achievement, various scholarship funds, ad infinitum. Life was good.

3
Finding God

Life As I Know It Ends . . .

My wife, Barbara, was a beautiful person, inside and out. More importantly, my wife was loved by everyone. She made everybody feel special. She never judged anyone. In fact, she appeared to not have an opinion about anything, and that was her problem. She had become so accustomed to suppressing her opinions and feelings that she was always slightly depressed. I loved my wife, who believed in God, more than words can express. It was her untimely death that led me back to God.

She took pleasure in things, most notably our children and their development, but she never seemed to experience joy. At least, not until the end. Whenever we would take the girls to an amusement park, the children and I would go on the rides, but Barbara would always opt to hold the coats, camera, and our other stuff instead of putting them in a storage locker and joining us. It was as if she used them as an excuse not to enjoy herself. She said she derived her pleasure from watching us.

Her parents had her late in life, and they doted on her as a child. They wouldn't let her ride a bicycle because she might get killed. They held off letting her get a driver's license because she might get killed. They butted in and tried to control every aspect of her adult life to the point of even interfering with our married life. Barbara kept most of this secret from me. Her parents destroyed her self-confidence with over-protectiveness and saw Barbara as fragile.

She was an excellent wife and mother, devoted to her family. I think she made a secret pact with herself to not raise her children in the same sort of suffocating atmosphere that she had been raised in. She went to great lengths to solicit our daughters' opinions. She shared in their thoughts, and encouraged them. She encouraged them to think for themselves, which, in my opinion, is the greatest gift a parent can give a child. She talked about opportunities with them for self-expression, and then, with their enthusiasm roused to try new things, she enrolled them in swimming, art, ballet, modern dance classes, gymnastics, and taught them to ride bikes at a young age. She encouraged any activity the girls expressed an interest in, and Barbara made sure the girls heard "I love you" from her on a daily basis.

Barbara was a professional homemaker. She had always wanted to be a homemaker, and even though she had a nursing degree, both of us wanted her at home providing for and raising the family. She loved to clean and nurse and cook, and she taught these skills to her daughters.

I worried because she seemed so dependent on her parents. She would not make even a simple decision without asking her mother's advice, and her mother was always at the ready to tell her what to do, think, and feel. In fact, her parents had insisted that she attend nursing school so she could "Save our lives when we become old and infirm."

Barbara suffered from what I call "The S'Mother Syndrome," that is, being "smothered by Mother." As parents, we need to control our babies' actions because they can't take care of themselves. They don't understand danger and death, like cars in the street. So our brain has to control two bodies, at least until they reach about ten. A wonderful thing happens then. Children start to think for themselves. They've learned to stay out of the street by then and maybe can be trusted to cross the street by themselves. But we have a ten-year habit built up. We've been taking responsibility for them and now it's hard to let go and let them start to fend for themselves.

After all, we reason, there is so much more they don't know about that can kill them or at least harm them in some way. It is an easy transition from being responsible for their very lives to being responsible for their very happiness. Our own fears make us fearful for them. We fear their potential failure in life. We fear for their successes. And we want to help. How much help do they need? How long shall we do their thinking for them?

Disaster struck when Barbara's mother contracted diabetes in her 70s. Barbara, the professional nurse, dutifully administered her mother's daily injections. A year later, the doctor discovered inoperable cancer in her mother and gave her maybe weeks to live. Barbara was crushed. She had killed her mother, or so she thought. She remembered back to her nurses' training that when an old person comes down with diabetes, it's *not* necessarily diabetes, but a harbinger of cancer.

She thought that if she had remembered this lesson, the doctors might have been able to catch the cancer in time. She was wracked with guilt. She left our home and moved into her mother's home to attend to her every need. When her mother finally had to go into the hospital for her last days, Barbara moved in with her, taking the bed next to her, living there day and night. When her mother finally died seven weeks later, Barbara was an emotional mess. She blamed herself, and no amount of explanation, logic, or reasoning could dissuade her from her guilt.

She sadly confided in me that now with her mother dead, she would never realize her life's dream. When I asked what that was, she said, "I've been waiting all of my life to hear my mother say 'I love you.' Just once." I was shocked. I hadn't realized that before. Yet I had never heard my mother-in-law say those three words to her, even once.

I tried to reassure her that her mother *did* love her. Maybe she wasn't very good at saying it, but all of her doting and interactions with her daughter proved that. It wasn't enough. I think Barbara interpreted her mother's doting *not* as an expression of love, but that her mother did not *believe* in her or her abilities as a woman and loving mother. Her mother had not trusted her with anything or any opinion. So, Barbara had learned to not trust herself, and she suppressed all her own opinions.

She began to sink into herself day by day after that. One day, she asked me why I always seemed to be so full of joy, life, and enthusiasm no matter how tough things were. She wanted to know how I could always bounce back in the face of adversity.

I had never thought about that before. I was hard pressed to explain my personality. Eventually it dawned on me that I had always felt loved by my mother. My mother had always solicited my opinion from as early as I can remember, and she was always encouraging of my thoughts and opinions, no matter how infantile. I began to recognize the damage Barbara's mother had done to her daughter. I also began to understand Barbara's dedicated devotion to not making that same mistake with her own daughters.

After a time, I started noticing patterns. Barbara would wear the same old clothes around the house day after day. Meals that she prepared, that heretofore had been culinary delights, became hot dogs and beans day in and day out. I confronted her and asked what the problem was. That's when she asked me to go for a walk so we could be alone. She confided in me that she had been seeing psychologists and psychiatrists for the past two years. She apologized that she had spent all of our life's savings on them, but announced that they had convinced her that she needed to be committed to a mental institution.

I was shocked. That was nonsense, I reasoned with her. I reminded her of how much she was loved by me, the children, and all our friends. I reasoned how her self-doubts were unfounded, *told* her what a wonderful and loving person she was, all to no avail. She was convinced she was a loser, and her doctors were convinced she was mentally ill. There was nothing I could say to unravel her false self-impression. Remember Barbara was a trained nurse, and to some nurses, doctors are like gods. She had been conditioned to think that doctors never made a mistake.

The next day she checked herself into a mental hospital. She rapidly deteriorated after that. I didn't learn, until after she died, that she had attempted suicide in the hospital. As Barbara sank, I was beside myself with worry and confusion about what I could do to help her. I would go to the hospital before work, during lunchtime, and after work, and stay long past visiting hours were over until they threw me out. Then I would go home and feed my children and bundle them off to bed. The stress and the long days began to take their toll on me. Work began to slide. I was neglecting my Naval Reserve duties. Our preteen children must have been perplexed as they saw the family unit dissolving before their eyes. They were fearful, and wanted to know where their mother was. I explained, as best I could.

Then my boss started making more demands on me, increasing my

66 hours of work per week. I pleaded for understanding, saying that I couldn't spend more time at work because I had to take care of my family, which was going through hard times. Of course, my employer knew all about my wife's incarceration in the mental hospital.

Barbara's doctors said maybe a change of scenery might help. Could I take a vacation? I had accumulated six weeks of vacation time over the previous three years and asked Barbara where she wanted to go. London? Phoenix? She protested that we couldn't afford that. But, to my mind, I would have spent anything to get my wife back. She settled on an in-state resort.

My company was not sympathetic. They said I was too valuable, and so they denied my leave request. I told my boss, "Look! My family comes first. Fire me if you want, but I'm taking my wife on vacation. The doctors recommend it, and I'm doing it!" I stormed out. I arranged for my mother to take our children, and I packed my wife into the car, and off we went for six weeks of sunshine and laughter. We weren't gone two days when my boss tracked me down. He threatened that if I didn't return immediately, I wouldn't have a job to come back to. "It's okay," my wife said, "I'm not enjoying this trip anyway. Let's go back." I wavered. The mental hospital was costing $20,000 a month, and without my job and my employer's insurance coverage, we would sink into oblivion. Against my better judgment, I caved in and we returned and she went back into the hospital.

Next, it was the Navy's turn to take a bite out of me. My commanding officer said I was getting behind in my work and ordered me to devote more off-drill time to Navy projects. We wound up in a shouting match, whereupon I ripped my Lieutenant Commander boards off my shoulders and threw them at him shouting, "I quit!" I stormed out of his office.

"You can't quit!" he shouted back at me. "I'll have you court-martialed!"

I broke out in a rash all over my body. The itching was furious and constant. I made oatmeal and spread it all over my naked body, and lay on my bed waiting for the intense itching to stop. I went to a dermatologist. He said that what I had was caused by stress, that I had "burned off" the protective layer under my skin, and I would most likely suffer from this skin condition for the rest of my life. He gave me some cream to alleviate the itching.

Eventually, the hospital's psychiatrists ordered me to enter therapy to help my wife. I was desperate, ready to do anything to help her. At the first session, a doctor took me into his office and explained that I had to be mentally ill, too. "There's nothing the matter with me," I protested. But he continued to press his case. He blamed me for my wife's instability; he blamed American society; he blamed everything and everyone she had ever come in contact with, *except* her parents. He said that she would probably have to be incarcerated for the rest of her natural life, that they had no hope for her recovery. He said that she was a high suicide risk, and they would have to keep her under close supervision.

He continued to work on me to convince me that I was mentally unstable and that I, too, had to be incarcerated. I began to believe him. After all, he was a doctor, and a professional in these matters. Right there, in his office, I began to fall apart. I became convinced that he was right. "But my children," I pleaded with him, "What is to become of my children if both parents are confined?"

"The state will take them and place them in foster care, of course," he said matter-of-factly.

That was the last straw. I had a sensation of my brain breaking in two. I fell apart. My life, as I knew it, was over. I crumpled off the chair and fell to the floor. "Help me, please," I begged. "Please tell me this is not happening." He looked disdainfully down from his superior position in his chair, and told me to go home, pack a toothbrush, and report back for incarceration in the morning.

Emotionally, I crawled out of his office on my hands and knees, too beaten down to be able to stand. I crawled down the corridor of the hospital and down the sidewalk to the parking lot, gasping for air, not realizing I was hyperventilating. I reached up and pulled the door handle of my car open and crawled inside. I turned on the engine and turned the air conditioner on full blast, and put my mouth over the vent to get some air into me so I could calm down enough to drive. That seemed to work, and I drove home crying over the fate of my children, who were about to be parentless.

When I got home, I got into bed, still sobbing. I racked my brain over how my family could have come to such a sorry pass. I was blaming myself. I had no blame, per se, so my brain started inventing blame. I lay there in bed with my brain going back over the events of my life trying to find some hope, some way out of the nightmare. I was looking to see if there was any truth to what the doctors were saying about it being my fault.

As I reviewed the events of my life, I saw myself as a cheat and a failure. Proof? Why, I hadn't even graduated high school. That embarrassment haunted me my whole life. But, I argued with myself, I graduated college with honors. But then, my brain found the falsity in that. I had taken tests and passed courses in college without reading all of the required material. So, I was a cheat after all.

"But, but . . ." I argued with myself. "I became an officer and a leader in the Naval Reserve." "Oh, yeah," my darker side argued. "But you're on your way to a court-martial now, aren't you, Loser?"

I couldn't win this battle with myself. I looked over every major event in my life, and saw flaws everywhere I looked. My lovely wife had broken our engagement several times before I was able to convince her to marry me. More proof of what a fast-talking slime I was. But, looking for any redeeming feature in my worthless life, I had made two bright, beautiful children. My lower thoughts saw through that. It was my wife who had birthed them, and raised them so well. I was always at work. How much of a contribution had I actually made to their lives? Everywhere I looked, I saw flaws in my character. If there weren't any, I made them up, and felt sorry for myself.

I kept going over my life's events seeing errors everywhere. It was like watching a movie of my life. Faster and faster the movie spun. Finally, it started in on condemnation. My pillow became soaked with tears of self-pity. I was convinced that my life—our lives—were over, that I would have to check myself into the mental institution in the morning, and the state would take my children to an orphanage.

I gave up, and prayed to fall into a mind-numbing sleep. When I awoke the next morning, my first thought was a prayer that this had all been a nightmare, that the world was right again. I realized it wasn't. My pillow was soaked. I must have been crying all night long.

Again, my mind raced over the events of my life, seeing failure in every one. Again the memories and thoughts spun in a circle of condemnation. I became aware—reluctantly at first—of a little tear in the filmstrip. A pinpoint of light was trying to get my attention. At first, I refused to acknowledge it. As the events continued to spin, I couldn't ignore the little pinpoint. I turned my head to look at it and the room burst into light, and I saw an event in my life I had been overlooking.

Saving Grace

The event was magnificent, an event so pure, so perfect, that I could find no fault in my actions in it. I remembered it over and over again searching for a flaw, trying to find some way to distort it into something ugly, like I had with all of the other events of my life. But, I couldn't find anything wrong with it.

At the time I was employed as a shopping center marketing manager. It was my job to run entertainments in the mall and advertise them to draw customers into the mall. I worked hard to be the best marketing manager in the mall business in the nation, and had come close to achieving that goal. I considered my first Christmas season to be a bust. Retailers do 40 percent of their annual business during the six weeks of the Christmas shopping season. If they don't make their Christmas, they don't make their year. If they don't make their year in any given year, it can drive them out of business. The pressure was on, but I was up to it.

I held a Santa Claus parade my first year in the business that only drew in 2,000 people. I considered that a failure. I went to my boss and offered to resign. She laughed and said that 2,000 people was a good turnout. I argued that the downtown parade always drew about 20,000 people, so I must be a failure. She said that it was impossible for a mall to draw 20,000 people. I told her to keep my letter of resignation on file, and if I didn't bring in at least 20,000 the following Christmas, I would leave my job voluntarily.

The following Christmas I convinced our board of directors to take a chance and vote me quadruple my normal Christmas decorations budget to allow me to spend $100,000. I promised them they would see a commensurate return on their investment, which meant I was promising them an additional $1 million in extra sales.

I bought a decorations package called "Walt Disney's Magic Kingdom of Christmas" that included a three-story Cinderella Castle, 50 animated figurines, a Seven Dwarfs Diamond Mine tableau, a Gepetto's Cottage complete with life-sized automatons of Gepetto, Pinocchio, Jiminy Cricket, Figaro, Cleo, and the Blue Fairy. Then I went over budget and spent $1,000 to have a Prince Charming costume made, and another $1,000 to have Cinderella's dress made, and hired two opera singers to wear the costumes and stroll through the mall singing *When You Wish upon a Star* and *Someday My Prince Will Come.*

I also arranged for a fireworks display to be set off over the mall—a half-hour of nothing but grand finale explosions for ten times the normal cost of an Independence Day display. I hired the best Santa Claus in the entertainment industry—one who had his own real Santa beard. I contracted with Disney's coloring book publisher to create a full-sized coloring book for Santa to give away free to his little visitors. It turned out that the hardest part was getting an instrumental version of those Disney songs as backup for the opera singers, but I convinced a museum to make a tape recording of the only existing versions.

I tried to get eight real reindeer to pull Santa's sleigh through the mall for the parade, but the week before the event, some poacher had slipped into their pen in Michigan and killed all of the reindeer with arrows. I was able to arrange for Mickey Mouse, Minnie Mouse, Donald Duck, Goofy, and Pluto characters from Disney World to put in an appearance in my opening night parade.

There. I had it. The perfect Christmas promotional event. But no matter how well an event was put together, if no one knew about it, it would flop. So next I put together a previously unheard of advertising campaign for the mall industry. I spent an additional $50,000—triple the normal budget—putting together an advertising campaign to run television commercials throughout the entire state of Wisconsin, as well as full-page, full-color newspaper ads and radio spots.

In the mall industry, I had learned that once we launched an ad campaign, we'd get a few phone calls from people inquiring about the entertainment. Every phone call represented about 2,000 people who would show up for the event. So, we would get about 1, 2, or 3 calls for a major event. When we got 22 phone calls for the Magic Kingdom of Christmas, I called the local Police Department and Sheriff's Department and warned them that we were expecting more than 40,000 customers to turn out for our Santa Arrival event. One of those calls was from an oil millionaire in Texas asking how his kids, whom he was going to fly up to Wisconsin in his private jet, could find the mall from the airport. I knew then that we had a winner on our hands. The cops scoffed and muttered something about how PR guys exaggerate.

The night of the event, 150,000 people descended on the shopping center. The mall could only hold about 40,000 people comfortably. 50,000 crammed into the mall and created a disaster. People were jammed nose to back. When the malls were filled, people crushed into the stores for standing room knocking over displays and trampling merchandise under foot. They stood in the fountain in the center court with water up to their ankles and their kids balanced on their shoulders. The maintenance crews turned off the escalators and visitors hung from the rails.

That left about 100,000 outside unable to get in. When the traffic jammed up on the streets ten miles in all directions and five miles on the freeway, people abandoned their cars on lawns or in the street and walked to the mall. Worse, for me, there was no room for my Santa parade with all of the Disney characters to move through the malls. We snaked the celebrities through the back delivery corridors and burst out into the center court pushing our way through the crowds.

The night was a disaster. Everybody was either disappointed or angry. The stores did no business that night, having had to close their store gates to keep the crowds out. The police, who had failed to call out their reserves until it was too late, were worried about a riot. The customers who had driven over 100 miles and couldn't get in were livid. I had to take out a full-page advertisement in *The Milwaukee Journal* apologizing to the public for their disappointment.

I had set an industry record for the turnout. I called Disney Productions and got permission to keep Mickey Mouse for the balance of the Christmas season to assuage those customers who could then come back and see what they had missed opening night. The bottom line was our Magic Kingdom of Christmas eventually brought in an additional $40 million in sales that season—a 36 percent increase over the previous season's average.

Sanity!

As I remembered this success, things started to fall into place. The world—my world—started to turn itself right-side up again. "Wait a minute. I graduated from high school. Maybe it was only a GED, but it was a graduation nonetheless. And I *did* graduate college cum laude on my *own* efforts. And I *am* an officer in the Naval Reserve, and a damned good one at that. This is all crap! There's nothing wrong with me. I don't have to listen to those loser, mind-bending doctors. They certainly aren't of any help to me or my wife. Screw them! I'm not committing myself. I've got a family to raise. And a wife to rescue from that funny farm." I decided to fight back.

I leapt from the bed and rushed to the telephone. I called the doctor who had devastated me the night before. "I'm not coming in this morning." I announced. "I don't need you or your so-called help. Take your nut-farm and stuff it! I've got a family to raise."

"Oh, no, Mr. Tucker," he moaned, "you're mentally ill and you need our care," he soothed.

I realized that all I had done was doubt myself and lose my confidence. Once I started believing in myself again, and stopped feeling sorry for myself, I came back to being me. I never looked back after that. I just assumed, as I had before I bought into all of the psychiatrists' mumbo-jumbo, that whatever happened I could figure things out for myself. Unfortunately, my wife, who put full faith in doctors, couldn't accept that her psychiatrists could be wrong, rejected any sense of self-confidence, and continued to believe that her doctors were right when they told her that she was incurably mentally ill.

I realized what they had subjected my wife to. I had to get her out of there. But only she could sign herself out. It took a long time, but I convinced her to at least sign herself out for a weekend visit at home. At last, a ray of light was cutting through our nightmare.

When I picked her up, she was virtually catatonic. She moved like a zombie, staring straight ahead and not responding to anything anybody said. I laid her down on our bed and she stared at the ceiling without any signs of life. Desperate, I racked my brain for what I could say to get through. Then it dawned on me. I could pray for her out loud. I felt a fraud, being an atheist, but I knew *she* believed, so I thought that might get through to her. I knelt down beside the bed, folded my hands, and prayed out loud. I stayed there praying for six hours without result. Then she sat bolt upright.

"Bill! I'm back!" she exclaimed. "I could hear you praying as if you were a million miles away. I didn't feel like I was in my body. Thank God you stuck with it. You got me back."

Life the rest of that weekend was almost normal. She cooked, she cleaned, she even sang while doing it. I tried to explain to her there was nothing wrong with her, that she had just lost her confidence and the doctors weren't helping her get it back. She was still convinced she was mentally ill, and nothing I said could dissuade her. After all, she reasoned, the doctors had told her she was sick, and doctors are never wrong. I talked and talked and talked, but I couldn't reach her. At least I made her promise that she would not return to the mental institution, but would stay at home, and if she felt medical help was still called for, she could go as an out-patient, *but with me along.*

Monday morning, I went to work. She called me before noon to tell me that her psychiatrist had called her at home wondering where she was, and had convinced her to return to the hospital, which was where she was calling me from. I was devastated. How was I going to wrench her from their grip?

All week long, I was a nervous wreck. Every once in a while, sitting at my office desk or in a meeting, my body would start to shake. If I was in a staff meeting, I excused myself, rushed to a phone, and called my wife at the hospital, convinced she was slipping downward and away. Sure enough, she'd be in the doldrums. I would talk soothingly to her, and slowly but surely build her confidence back up. I didn't hang up until I was sure she was okay, for the moment. Sometimes I would be sitting at my desk and would think about her until I worked myself up into a frenzy and would call her. But she'd be okay. Then the next time my body started to shake, I'd call, and she would be down again, and again I'd talk her back up.

The next weekend, I was able to convince her to sign herself out on a weekend pass. The previous weekend, she and I had agreed that maybe if she had a job outside the home it might take her mind off her falsely based self-pity. I had lined up a job interview for her for the following Monday morning. Sunday night I got her to agree again not to return to the hospital. I left for work the next morning.

At about two o'clock in the afternoon, as I sat writing at my desk, an unexplainable force slammed me on the left side from the direction of the wall. A moment later I found myself 12 feet from my desk, lying on the floor and wondering what the hell had hit me. No one else was in the room. Dazed, the first thought that shot across my mind was, "Barbara's dead. Oh my god, my wife just died!" I felt like I had been torn in two. "No . . . no . . . that couldn't be," I thought. "I'm just scaring myself again."

I got up off the floor and returned to my desk, and the task at hand. Several hours later, my eldest daughter called me at work. "Where's Mom?" she asked.

"Isn't she there?" I stammered.

"No, but the meat is out of the freezer, thawing on the kitchen counter," she reported.

"Well, she's got to be there somewhere," I reasoned. "Look around the house."

"I have, Dad. She's nowhere to be found."

"Well, just wait. She probably had to run to the store for something."

Then it hit me. "What am I saying?! I must be an idiot. If something terrible *did* happen to her, I can't let my daughter find her body." I dialed my brother-in-law who lived a mile away. I was 17 miles away and in charge of a two-level enclosed mall shopping center. I was the manager-on-duty that night and couldn't leave.

"Dick, rush over to my house," I told my brother-in-law, "and look for Barbara."

"Why?" he asked.

"I don't know, but I'm worried about her. Please, rush over and see if she needs any help," I ordered, and hung up. "What am I doing?" I asked myself. "This is my wife. Screw the shopping center, the job, all of it. I have to be there for my wife."

I picked up the radio phone and called mall security. "You're in charge. I have to leave right now!" I jumped into my car, put the pedal to the floor, and sped home, running red lights, stop signs, swerving around traffic. The ambulance, with her lifeless body, was pulling away from the front of my house as I pulled up. I fell to pieces. My life ended at that moment, never to be the same again. I railed against God, country, cops, coroner, anybody and everybody within earshot. My lovely, sweet wife was dead.

Much later, I discovered that she had died at two in the afternoon, the same time I was knocked across the room, and on the six-month anniversary of her mother's death. Barbara had written a poem expressing her utter despair at having to live without her mother, and not being able to. I found this later.

Everything Ends

Family and friends rushed to be at our side and helped us through the funeral. The other officers of my Naval Reserve unit showed up in full dress uniform to be the pallbearers. Then they were gone and we were left alone. I asked my mother to move in with us and stay for a while to help hold everything together. She organized the household, made meals for us, and tried to cheer us up, but there was no room in any of our hearts for that. Eventually, when I convinced her that we were stable, she left.

I went back to work. My boss had the audacity to come into my office and flippantly say, "Well, that's behind you now. Time to get on with your life." I lost it and shouted, "You bastard! You and this stinking company helped kill my wife by not letting me take the vacation I had coming, and now you want to make light of it?"

"You're fired," he said, "Clear out your desk. You've got 15 minutes to vacate your office."

That week, I received a letter from my former employer's health insurer. "We are sorry to inform you that your former health policy only covers physical ailments, not mental, so we will not be able to pay the $60,000 mental hospital bill. This is now your responsibility. Please pay it promptly to avoid any further discomforts."

I called my bank to see about getting a loan against my home to pay the debt. They informed me that they were sorry, but it seemed my wife had mortgaged the home. "Oh, and by the way, you are months behind in your new house payments." They wanted to know when they could have their money.

I was in a malaise. My wife was gone. My career was gone. My health was gone (still itching). The Navy was gone. My money was gone. And now my children and my home were about to be gone. My friends and family had returned to their daily concerns. I called a few friends to see if I could garner any help from them, but I was shocked at the reception I got. It seemed that now that I was a single man, they felt threatened that I might come after their wives, so I was no longer welcome and they hung up on me. I was dying inside, missing my wife more than words can describe, and friendly doors were slamming shut.

I called the county welfare department. "I need some money to save my home and my kids. My wife just died, and I'm out of work, and in debt up to my ears," I reported.

"Do you own a car, and furniture, and any other assets?" they asked.

"Of course."

"Well, sell them off, use the money you get to live on, and, when that's all gone, we'll give you $400 a month welfare money."

"Hey! Wait a minute! I've been paying taxes all my life. It's time the government paid me something back, in my hour of need." I argued.

"I'm sorry, we only help those who are destitute, and since you have assets . . ." she trailed off.

"But . . . but . . . the whole idea is to save my house, and my kids." I implored.

"Oh, you don't have to worry about your children," she replied, "Since you can't provide a decent home, the state will take them from you, as an unfit father, and place them in foster care. They will be well taken care of."

On my sofa, I stared out the window. There was nothing to do now but wait for "them" to come and take everything away.

I was mad. The race was over and I had lost everything, and I was angry as hell about it! It wasn't fair. We had gone from being a happy, successful family to destruction in a matter of months. I needed somebody to blame. I turned the events over in my mind. I hated my employer for trashing my family when I needed my job the most. I hated their health insurance company. I turned my attention to my commanding officer and the Navy. It was their fault for not backing me in my time of tribulation. But that wasn't enough. The psychiatrists! Those were the bastards that caused all of this to happen. Even collectively they were not enough to absorb the anger and hate that seethed within me. It was *me* who had let my wife down, I finally realized. It must be *my* fault. But I couldn't eat that lie, either. I knew how much I loved and adored her, and how hard I tried to help. There was no one to blame.

Huge Shoulders

I sat there, trying to think of what I could do next. I did not want to go on living. I ached to crawl into a grave next to my wife and be with her in the Hereafter. Except the problem was I didn't believe in life after death. I was an atheist, remember.

The only solution was to kill myself. At least my children would inherit my life insurance and I would be out of my pain and this stinking life. (Depressed people never consider the negative impact such an action will have on their loved ones remaining behind.) Still the anger seethed. I needed to vent. I had to get it out or I would burst. I looked up at the ceiling. I knew One big enough to dump my hate onto.

"You bastard!" I shouted out loud at my ceiling. "I don't know if You are up there, but *if* You are, I'm telling You that you are a poor excuse for a god. If You were mad at me for being an atheist, then why didn't You kill me? Why kill the one person who trusted You and loved You so much? Why hurt our children by depriving them of their mother, who, thanks to their mother, also believe in You? You are a filthy, stinking, rotten S.O.B.! You bastard . . . *You killed my wife!*"

The ceiling said nothing.

I stared out the window.

"That's it," I thought to myself, again. "The only solution to all of my problems is that I have to die!" I looked back up at my ceiling.

"Well, You piece of crap, God, You, You miserable, stinking S.O.B. I'm not sticking around to feel *this* pain for the next 40 years! I'm outa here! Screw You, and all Your faith crap. I'm taking my life, and then I'll be dead. No Afterlife. Just out of this pain and agony. I can't bear it any longer. I'm going to starve myself to death, and there is *nothing* You can do about it. You can't stop me because I am more powerful than You, You phony excuse for a god. All-loving, *indeed*. Go to hell, Yourself!" I was really giving it to my ceiling.

The ceiling was silent.

4

The Formula for Getting Miracles

Miracles . . .

I continued to rant and rave with my plan. "I will not eat for the next three weeks," I announced out loud to my ceiling. "Then I will die of starvation. The kids can eat at friends' homes. They're hardly home anymore, anyway. This is certainly not a fun place to be. This is where their mother died, You bastard! Besides, I don't have any food in the house, and no money to buy any with. I'll tell You what. I'll show You just how puny You are. I don't care if You deliver supper to my front door every day for the next three weeks. I'm not eating! I don't care if supper shows up on my doorstep at five o'clock every day. I don't eat. I die. The game is over. I'm finally done with Your hole of a stinking world."

I hesitated for a moment. Why did I just say five o'clock, I wondered? After all, we didn't eat until six P.M., ordinarily. Oh, well, what difference did it make? I shrugged it off.

The kids came home from school. My plan was in place. I would allow myself to have all of the coffee with cream and sugar in it, and all of the cigarettes I wanted, to ease the starvation pains, but food was out of the question.

Free Food–The First Miracle

At five o'clock that day, the doorbell rang. It was April, who lived across the street. She was holding a pot. "What do you want, April?" I snapped.

"Well, I feel so bad about Barbara and all . . . well . . . I've made supper for you and the girls," she said, extending the pot.

"If you want to feed the kids," I answered her, "they're in the other room, but I'm not eating." April came in, and fed the girls, washed her pot and the dishes, and left.

I sat on the sofa all the next day, staring out the window, feeling sorry for myself, waiting to die.

At five o'clock that second day, my doorbell rang. It was a stranger I had never seen before.

"Hello, Mr. Tucker," she smiled. "You don't know me, and I don't know you, but I used to attend church with your lovely wife, and I feel so bad about your tragedy, that I wanted to do something for you. So, I've made supper for you and your children." She held out a pot of food.

"Well, the kids are in the other room, but I'm not eating." She came in and fed the girls, washed her pot and the dishes, and left.

The next day, at the stroke of five P.M., my doorbell rang again. There was yet another woman I didn't know standing on my stoop holding a pot.

"Are you Mr. Tucker?" she asked. "You don't know me, and I don't know you, but I live two blocks over, and I felt so bad when I heard about your tragedy that I wanted to do something nice for you and your children, so I've made supper for you." She thrust a pot of food at me.

"If you want to feed the kids, they're in the other room, but I'm not eating," I said. She came in, fed the girls, washed her pot and the dishes, and left.

The fourth day, the doorbell rang at five P.M. I answered it, and it was still another woman I didn't know. She had the same message and so did I.

"Do you go to our church?" I asked bitterly, thinking that maybe there was a conspiracy of sorts being played out in the neighborhood.

"Oh, no, I go to the Catholic Church over on Loomis," she said. I didn't know any Catholics in the neighborhood, so I took her at her word.

The same thing happened the fifth, sixth, and seventh days, and for the next two weeks, all strangers appearing at five o'clock carrying food. None of this registered with me. I didn't think anything of it. Just do-gooders butting in, was my self-pitying attitude. I spent my days sitting on my sofa staring out the window, waiting to die of starvation.

By the 18th day of these visits, I was perplexed. I was nowhere near dying. I had only lost about 25 pounds and was starting to look trim. I wondered how long it would take to die of starvation. Slowly, the light started to come on in my head. What *was* this? Why were these women showing up on my doorstep with food? "But," I thought, "wait a minute. *I'm* the one who said, 'supper at my door at five o'clock.' Nobody else heard me say that to my ceiling. It couldn't be . . . could it? Naw, now I'm losing my mind. Just a coincidence."

The unanswered questions hung heavy. I said to the ceiling, "What is this? Is this some sort of miracle demonstration? A couple of free meals, and You call *that* a miracle! Go to hell! Keep Your food! You want to get me back? Get Barbara out of the ground. Raise her from the dead, like you did Lazarus and Jesus and that little girl and so many others reported in the Bible. *Then* You get me back. *Then* I'll believe in miracles. In the meantime, I'm not eating . . . I die . . . I win by escaping from this hellhole You call a 'world' . . . and *You* lose. Because . . . I . . . am . . . more . . . powerful . . . than . . . You."

The ceiling didn't respond, of course.

On the 19th day, I peeked out my living room drapes at five minutes before five o'clock. There was a little old lady toddling down the street toward my house carrying a pot. I watched my wristwatch. One minute to go, as she passed the house next door. Bing-bong, went the doorbell at the very stroke of five P.M. We exchanged the same words that had happened every day for the past three weeks. She came in, fed the girls, washed the dishes, and left. I sat and watched in amazement.

The 20th day I didn't even bother to look out the window. I stood by the front door at one minute to five P.M. staring at my watch, wondering if it was fast or slow, wondering why the doorbell always rang when *my* watch read five o'clock. At five seconds before the stroke of five, I pulled the door open, and saw another stranger step up and reach for the bell.

After she left, I thought about the events of the past weeks. "This goes way beyond coincidence," I thought. "But it can't be a miracle; there haven't been any miracles for two thousand years. Have there? I *must* be losing my mind. That's it. I'm over the edge. Delirious from lack of food." I couldn't shake the feeling that I was living in some sort of a twilight zone. I needed answers. I rushed around the house looking for our medical dictionary. I looked up starvation. It said that the human body could go without food for two months, but a person could die from dehydration in three weeks. I flashed back on all of the pots of coffee I had been drinking, laced with sugar and milk—glucose—the substance of life.

"What an idiot I've been," I thought to myself. "Okay, this nonsense has gone on long enough." I looked back up at my ceiling, and said, "Okay, if You're up there, listen up. I was wrong. I can't die in three weeks from starvation. But I can and surely will die if I don't eat for three months. So, that's the new plan. I'm not eating for the next three months whether You deliver food to my doorstep at five o'clock, or not. Then, surely I will die, and You will lose, and I will be out of my pain and agony, so I will finally *win*." I felt like cackling hysterically, but thought that a bit over-dramatic, so I didn't.

The next day, a Saturday, and the 21st day since my ordeal began, the doorbell rang at five o'clock. I pulled the door open, and stared at the man standing there dressed in white: white shirt, white work pants, and sporting a little black bowtie. I looked past him to his white panel truck. It had a black bowtie logo painted on it, and it read, "Ron's Catering."

"Hi. I'm Ron of Ron's Catering," he announced. "All of your former employees and friends at the shopping center feel very bad about your loss. They wanted to do something nice for you, so they took up a collection and raised $5,000. They didn't want to just give you the money. They thought that would be too crass. So, they've hired me to bring you and your children supper every day for the next three months. Is five o'clock okay?"

I was dumbfounded. How could this *be*? I can't be hearing this. I'm the one who said to my ceiling three months. I'm the one who said five o'clock. And then it struck me: I couldn't win this contest of wills. No matter what I said or did, the food was going to keep on coming. I laughed hysterically, tears streaming down my face. I opened the door wider, and with a sweeping motion of my arm, bade my visitor in. He set a silver tray down on the table and announced, "Don't bother to wash our dishes. We take them back dirty and sterilize them in our kitchens." And with that he left.

I looked at the ceiling, and said, "Okay. You win. I'll eat." I called the girls, and we shared a meal together for the first time in weeks.

The next morning, with renewed vigor, I plopped down on my sofa to stare out the window and think about what was next. I was still in ruin. I owed the mental institution $60,000, and was being dunned for payment—an amount I figured I couldn't save in three lifetimes *if* I had a job. The house was on its way out from under me, the kids were about to be taken from me, and I was expecting to be ordered to court-martial by the Navy any day. And that itching was unabated.

Any way I thought about it, there seemed to be no solution at hand. My life was still to be a wretched experience, full of the pain of losing my wife. Then a selfish thought crossed my mind. I looked up at that wonderful, silent ceiling, and said, "Okay, Big Guy. You made this mess I am in, and You dug this pit for me, and You are making me stay alive, so You fix it. Put $60,000 in my mailbox over the next 30 days. If You can deliver three months and three weeks of free food to my doorstep, a mere $60,000 should be easy for You." I demanded it.

Free Money–The Second Miracle

The next day, when I went to my mailbox, I found a single envelope with a check for $500. Seems it was a rebate, of some sort, for something we had purchased some time in the past that I had no recollection of. I accepted that unquestioningly.

The next day there was again one envelope in my mailbox. In it was a check from an old Air Force buddy for $2,000. The enclosed letter read, "Dear Bill, here is the $1,000 you loaned me 20 years ago, with another $1,000 for interest. Thanks a lot!" I had forgotten about that loan.

The next day, again, one envelope. This time it was a letter from the Internal Revenue Service. It seems I had made a mistake on my taxes ten years before and had overpaid my taxes. Enclosed was a check for $5,000. The first thought that flew through my mind was, I thought the IRS only went back seven years in their records.

Every day after that, there was always just one envelope in my mailbox. There was never any junk mail or bills, and every envelope had some money in it, small amounts, large amounts. For example, I won a radio station contest I didn't remember entering. By the 29th day, I had collected $15,000 from my mailbox. How could this be? If I was certain of anything, it was that I would have the whole $60,000 by the next day, the last day of the month I had given God to deliver the money.

On the 30th day, I went to my mailbox, and drew out the one envelope that was in there. I opened it, and found a letter and a check. The check was for $45,000 from my former employer's health insurer. It read in part, "Dear Mr. Tucker, in reviewing your medical claim for your wife's recent illness, we note that some mental illnesses are caused by a chemical imbalance in the brain. A chemical imbalance could be interpreted as a physical, not strictly mental, condition. Inasmuch as your wife has passed on, and a determination of the cause cannot now be made, we have decided to err on the side of a chemical imbalance physical cause. Enclosed, please find our check for 75 percent of your wife's hospital bill. We hope that this has not inconvenienced you in any way."

I was stunned . . . but, and here's the important part . . . not *surprised!* I fully *expected* to find that check in my mailbox, although I had no idea from where it would come.

5

How to Get Miracles

"Aladdin's Magic Lamp"

Breathing room! I paid off the mental institution bill. "Now," I said, on familiar terms with my ceiling, "We . . . er, You have to do something to finish saving the house. I need some operating cash to make the payments on the loan Barbara borrowed against the house." Then *I put it out of my mind* (one of the most significant things I have ever done in my life), as I returned to my familiar place on the sofa, and stared out the window again, to contemplate this strange turn of events.

The next day I received another envelope in my mailbox. This time it was from my former employer. In it was a form letter telling me that I had accumulated $50,000 in my fully vested retirement fund, and, since I was no longer an employee, a check for that amount was enclosed.

I was living in a dream world. Everything seemed to have turned to crap, yet now, just for the asking, everything was turning around for me. The kids were safe. The house was safe. I could get on with my life. I felt myself healing emotionally from the loss of my wife as I started to make plans and be a father to my precious children again. My Navy commanding officer called to apologize, and to tell me that he had not acted on my "insubordination," and that I was welcome back. I started going to my monthly drill meetings again.

My body started to heal. The rash subsided over 90 percent of my body. I gave credit to God and to the lower stress levels I was experiencing, but I knew where all the credit belonged. I had prayed every day for

34

the rash to go away permanently. But it's interesting the form my prayers took. I didn't ask God for healing *every day*. That seemed unnatural to me. After all, if you ask once, isn't that enough? I reasoned that if you ask a second time, isn't that indicating that you didn't believe it would happen the first time you asked? Maybe there wouldn't be any sincerity the second time, either. The way I prayed was to just say, "Thank you for healing me, Father!" I didn't even bother to look for signs of the healing. Why should I? If I itched, I applied the doctor's cream and *assumed* that God would work the miracle in God's own time.

I spent the next year applying for jobs, only to be turned down regularly. It became apparent to me that anyone over 40 was going to have a tough time finding work. Then I tried a couple of entrepreneurial efforts that failed. I had set up a college fund for each of my children and had been living off the balance of my retirement money. It was nearly all gone. I was now back on my sofa staring out the window, wondering what my next move should be.

I thought to myself, "Why me? Me, of all people. I hadn't been a *believer*. There are plenty of people trucking on down to their local church every Sunday asking for miracles, and not getting them. Why should I be singled out? Those people deserve a miracle for the demonstration of their faithfulness, not *me*. I was a heathen. Why would God have deigned to answer *my* prayers?" What was next in this strange series of events happening *to* me, not *because* of me?

The question plagued me. I had to have an answer. I rushed through the house looking for my wife's Bible. Maybe the answer was in there. I decided to read it cover to cover until I found an answer. I had opened it a few times in my childhood, but had quickly put it down again, the language too hard to follow. When, as a young adult, I was looking into various religions, the Bible turned me off because there was so much judgmental stuff about God killing some people in answer to other people's prayers. It didn't seem right to me. But now I was on a mission. I read the Bible all the way through, yet without finding what I was looking for. What I *did* discover was that it wasn't that hard to understand. I determined to read it again.

On the second reading, I still didn't find what I was looking for, but I learned something else. I learned that the Bible was a simple document to understand, so simple that a child could follow it if one made the effort. All the books of the Bible seemed to boil down to one message, and amazingly, the message was always the same: Believe in God.

But I still needed an answer to my question: Why me? So I read it a third time. This time I found it. There in Mark 11:22–25 was a "formula" for getting a miracle just for the asking. I realized why many people didn't get their miracles. They were only doing the first part of a three-part formula. As I reflected on my recent experiences, I saw I had inadvertently done all three. God had no choice. According to this passage, when one follows the instructions, God *promises* to grant the request.

It was obvious to me as a nonbeliever that if one faithfully applied the formula, one could not fail to be granted his wish because *God promised.* If it didn't happen, only one of two things could be true: Either there was no God, or God is a liar. Since neither is true, God *has* to come through. Aladdin's magic lamp! I was a *believer* again.

I pondered the bent-blade-of-grass request, and the request for the drops of rain to fall from a blue sky. I had not *believed* in advance, and that was the operative part of the formula. I was looking for God to give me proof that God existed. But the rule is, "Faith first, then proof." If merely asking for God to prove God's Self were enough, everybody would be a believer, and then faith and belief wouldn't be necessary. I didn't understand at the time why God had set up such a system. It wasn't until decades later, when I read God's thought behind the whole composition of life and the world in Neale Donald Walsch's trilogy of books, *Conversations With God,* that I understood this sublime and loving construct. All the Bible tells us is to believe in God over and over again. Apparently, we don't, ergo, the reason for the admonition.

Why me? Because, when I was talking to my ceiling (I envisioned that I was speaking directly to God, of course), I was giving God exactly what God required: belief. One doesn't talk to one not there, and I was sincere in my protestations.

So, what is the formula for getting miracles? It's very simple, and yet the hardest thing for mankind to do—trust in the impossible, the unexplainable, *in advance.* Here is how Mark (11:22–25 RSV) puts it:

And Jesus answered them, Have faith in God. Truly, I say to you, whoever says to this mountain, "Be taken up and cast into the sea," and does not doubt in his heart, but believes that what he says will come to pass, it will be done for him. Therefore, I tell you, whatever you ask in prayer, believe that you have received it, and it will be yours. And, whenever you stand praying, forgive, if you have anything against anyone; so that your Father also, who is in heaven, may forgive you your trespasses.

The formula then is:

1. Ask God for *anything* you want in prayer
2. Believe, *in advance* that it's *already* done
3. Forgive, in your heart, anyone you are judging

I discovered that it takes all three parts to have God work miracles for us. All believers seem to do step 1. But if we stop there, we will fail to get our miracle. Then likely we will blame God for having failed *us*, rather than the other way around.

Step 3, it seems to me, isn't strictly *required*. In the quoted passage, all that *is* required is to ask God for what you want and *truly* believe to the core of your heart in advance that it will happen; the promise is, it will be done unto you. In step 3, God never judges any of His children, and God certainly doesn't find any of them wanting. How could God? God created the world, so how could God hold us accountable for what God made?

Jesus, as one religion's example, says over and over, "Judge not, lest ye be judged." I interpret that as a two-part thought: (1) Don't judge others and (2) if you do judge others, God may judge *you*, and find you as wanting as the person *you* are judging. In another passage, Christ says something to the effect that only God and I may judge and We do not, so why do you? So, the second part of that admonition to "Judge not, lest ye be judged" seems to be just a scare tactic. It's designed to get our focus on the first part and see how useless it is, that judging others serves no great purpose. In fact, when we do judge others, aren't we acting "un-Godly" since God doesn't judge us?

Many people may cite examples of when it is necessary to kill, such as war or capital punishment. We may ask ourselves what is the purpose of capital punishment? When we as a society put a murderer to death, what are we saying? Killing is wrong, so you can't kill, but *we*, the "good" people, can? Do we not rationalize killing and assign value to the type of killing, and to who can or cannot do it? Are we not playing God with other people's lives, but don't want other people playing God in ours? Why is it important to take the life of another? To teach one a lesson? To serve as an example for other would-be murderers? Do either of these work? Has killing murderers stopped murders from happening? Have they ever? Maybe it's for vengeance, to make us feel good about paying them back. Does our killing a fellow human make us feel better?

If you are one of those who would defend killing a killer, it seems to me that two things must be true. First is the basic attitude that life is precious. Do we sanctify life and do everything we can to keep life going as long as possible? If so, why? Is this a race that can be won? Consider the soldier who survives years of war, only to step off the plane that brings him home to be killed by a drunk driver. How can we keep anyone alive for a moment beyond their intended death date set by God? If life could be extended *forever*, there might be a case to be made here. But, inasmuch as all people die eventually, isn't it more productive to spend our time on the quality of life instead of the quantity of days?

Second is that when we judge others, we are on the outside of God's desire. If that's where we are, how can God reward us with a miracle? Each of us must choose whether we want to be on the right hand of God getting our needs met and having miracles happen in our lives, or not. If jealousy, judgments, revenge, retribution, anger, and hate are more important to us than living in love with our fellow man, then that is how we are free to live. That is "free will." If God had offered *me* the apple in Paradise, I'd like to think that I'd have taken a pass. As it is, God didn't, and according to religion, I am tainted as a sinner from birth because someone else did. That's a fairy tale I can't subscribe to. After all, *my* God is an *all loving* God. God wouldn't have judged them and found them wanting, and God doesn't judge me.

Step 3 isn't easy, but it's doable if we put our heart and mind to it. Here's what I do: I rise above the issue of the moment and consider the source. "Consider the source" is an idiom meaning "consider the person from whom the objectionable is coming." In other words, instead of "judging" another, we should rise above the petty conflict and try to understand where the other person is coming from. It is better to pity them for their lack of understanding, and to rise above the judgment. All of mankind was made by God and are God's children; all of us are loving beings trying to get along in this world alone and fearful. Fearful of failure, of making a mistake, of being hurt physically or emotionally. Fearful of anything and everything. When I step back and focus on the fact that everybody is trying to do their best, it's easy to forgive, regardless of how stupidly or meanly they act.

Speaking of fear, listen to what people say. Someone might read this book, and say, "I'm afraid I can't believe what he is saying." They *are* afraid. They are afraid to believe it or they are afraid it is not true. The operative part of that statement seems to be "afraid." All mankind seems to be afraid, but of what? I think the big one is death. But more importantly, they are afraid that maybe God does not exist and we are here alone. How sad for them. How sad for us. How sad it was for me!

So step 2, believing in advance, I found nearly impossible to do or unbelievably easy. Impossible, because we put so much importance on the things that worry us. We want so desperately for something wonderful to happen (such as having a loved one saved from their cancer), that it becomes too wonderful to feel privileged to receive such a great gift. We pray and ask, but then our fear conquers us and we doubt. Obviously, that is not demonstrating faith, so our loved one dies, and we turn our anguish and blame on God.

But, also, step 2 is the easiest thing we can do when we disassociate ourselves from a particular outcome. That's why it is sometimes easier for an atheist to get a miracle. Since they don't believe in God and God's miracles, they don't bother to ask. They just resign themselves to the projected outcome, and let the chips fall where they may. All of a sudden their loved one's cancer goes away, and they are perplexed as to why. The "why" is because they didn't worry about or aggravate the issue. They "let go," and in so doing, they "let God!" by default.

Sometimes we want something so badly, so desperately, that we are just too afraid to "let go." And that is our undoing. Because that shows absolutely no faith in God coming across with what we desire.

6

Getting Miracles for
the Asking *and* Believing

Free Miracles

Let's return to the story of my accidental discovery of how miracles happen. I had experienced miracles and knew the formula. What should I do with this beneficence? Rub the magic lamp, of course. I was still out of work. I needed a job. But now I realized that I could have any job that my heart desired, just for the asking *and believing*.

Forgiveness

I had unfinished business to attend to. I had to get on the right side of God. I had a lot of forgiving to do. It wasn't easy, so first, I tackled the easy ones. I thought long and hard about my Naval Reserve commanding office and about the Navy; both, I felt, were insensitive to my family's plight and had contributed in some degree to my wife's death. It was simple to forgive the Navy. Institutions are made up of people, yet those people were not aware of my wife's plight. As for my commanding officer, it was easy to forgive him because of an incident that happened a couple days after the funeral.

Those were the worst days of my life. The pain of the loss of my wife was unbearable. I felt a weight crushing my chest, making it hard to breathe. The stress of it made me drop off to sleep in the middle of a sentence; I would awake moments later only to find the pain still with me. I wasn't thinking clearly, nor rationally. I was chain-smoking cigarettes and eating little.

My commanding officer, sympathetic now over the ultimate turn of events, and maybe feeling a little guilty, called me up one night. "Bill, I can appreciate what you are going through. A couple of years ago my wife left me. That was bad enough. But then my parents died shortly thereafter. My grandparents, on both sides, had also died some years before that. So, in a very short period, I went from having an extended, happy, and loving family, to being totally alone in the world. It was a crushing blow. One that I could not have survived had it not been for a friend of mine who called me up, and made me promise something, which is what I am going to make you promise to me.

"One night, soon, you will awake at three A.M. You will light a cigarette and sit in the dark reexperiencing the pain of your loss. You will cry. You will ponder the worth of continuing. You will decide to end it all and you will walk into the kitchen, take out a carving knife, and slit your wrists. When that night comes, I want you to promise me that you will *first*, before taking the knife out of the kitchen drawer, *call me* at that precise moment!"

I protested, "Phil, I'm all right," but, to be honest, I was already planning my suicide. "Besides, I'm not calling your house at three in the morning. You've got a baby there, and I'm not going to bother you with such foolishness and wake your baby." I lied through my teeth. "There," I thought, "I've put that out of my way. Now I'm free to kill myself."

A week later, I *did* awake at three A.M. I stumbled through the dark into the living room and lit a cigarette. I sat there in the dark reexperiencing the pain and focusing on the fact that I did not want to live without her. I cried. I decided I would not go on living. I walked into the kitchen and opened the knife drawer. I stared at the carving knife, sighed, and picked it up. Just then the phone rang. I glanced up at the clock. "Who can be calling me at three in the morning?"

It was my commanding officer. "Phil! Why are you calling me at three A.M.?" I demanded.

"More to the point," he said, "What are you doing up at three A.M.?"

"Nothing."

"Put the knife back in the drawer!" He demanded.

I stammered like a kid caught with his hand in the cookie jar, "Knife . . . er . . . what knife?"

"Look, Bill," he continued, "You're not the first person to go through this. We all need a little help from our friends and from God at a moment like this. Please put the knife back."

I did as he instructed. "How did you know that this was the night that I would be here at the kitchen drawer?"

"I didn't. I've been setting my alarm clock for three A.M. every night, getting up, and calling you. If you didn't answer by the third ring, then I knew it wasn't the night. I was determined to call every night until you answered. Now, go back to bed and never lie to me again."

I was humbled by his kindness. "You've saved my life."

"Just passing the miracle on, my friend, as it was done unto me."

Forgiving him was easy after that. But there were still my former boss and employer. I realized they didn't have a crystal ball and couldn't foresee the future any better than I could. I decided to consider the source, go into my heart, and forgive them their trespasses.

The psychiatrists were the most difficult to forgive. I discovered that psychiatrists lose 25 percent of their patients to suicide. Surgeons, in contrast, only lose about two percent of their patients on the operating table. I wasn't surprised. A lack of faith-based psychiatric help was obviously no help at all. But I didn't let go of my anger easily.

I visited a lawyer with the intent of suing the psychiatrists for wrongful death. I wanted those bastards to pay for killing my wife, for robbing her of her self-confidence. I didn't see this as a judgment at the time. The lawyer gave me a dose of reality. "You can sue them, if you want to put down a $30,000 retainer," he said. "But the most you can win is $50,000, according to state law. The psychiatrists' association lobbied the state senate and got that protection for their members. Moreover, you can't win because you'd have to find two psychiatrists to testify against your wife's doctors, and that isn't going to happen. They all protect one another."

I had no other choice but to look into my heart and find a way to forgive them. Really forgive them! After all, God would know if I was just giving it lip service. My new relationship with God was too important to let those jerks come between us. I finally forgave them by pitying them for their ignorance. I determined that, at some point in my life, I would help them to understand the errors they were making in trying to help people by stealing their patients' sense of self-worth.

When you realize that there is a God and that God loves us more than we can know, and takes care of us as we believe in God and God's power to do so, you have nothing to fear. Ultimately, you realize nothing matters, nothing save our faith in God. With that appreciation, how could anyone lose belief in oneself? As God loves me, I love me.

Time to Move On

It was time to get a job. On the sofa, I stared out the window, searching for what I wanted to do. I had always wanted to be an entrepreneur, but in what business? I had a lifelong love of advertising and publishing, but that would take money. How much? $50,000? $100,000? More than a year had passed since my last miracle, and I was broke again.

I said to my ceiling, "God, please deliver to me one million dollars, free and clear, in the next 14 days to start my business. I want to be the president of an advertising and/or publishing company."

I knew that it was a done deal. *I then put it out of my mind.* After all, the request was in, and the deed was as good as done. In fact, it *was* done! An hour later, the doorbell rang. (Are you getting chills? I did.) It was Russ, a friend of mine, who had also been let go a few months before me by the same employer. He said that if I didn't have a job, he'd like me to consider going into business with him. I asked what it was. He reached into his briefcase and pulled out a magazine mock-up.

"It's an advertising magazine," he said, "and I'd like us to publish it."

"Great!" I responded. "Let's do it!"

He said that he would like me to be president because we had worked together in the past, and even though he had once been my boss, he felt that I had more experience. I protested, but he was insistent, so I accepted. I smiled at the charm of how it all fell into my lap. There was only one thing left, and I had given God 14 days to do it.

"Okay, boss," he laughed, "What's our first order of business?"

I told him to go rent an office, order furniture, get a phone, advertise for employees, hire a law firm, and hire an accountancy firm. He wanted to know what I was going to do? "I will get the money to pay for it all, of course."

He asked how we were going to be able to get a law firm and accountants without cash up front. I told him to offer them a seat on our board of directors for no pay but a modicum of stock.

A week later, he was back. "Get in the car. I've got something to show you," he said. He drove me downtown, and we walked into our new offices, humming with activity. Men were carrying our new office furniture into the spaces and the phone company was hooking up the phones. He introduced me to our new secretary and to some prospective salesmen being interviewed. We sat down at our big, new desks and put our feet up.

Russ said, "Well, I got us one of the best-known law firms in town. I told the managing partner we wanted to engage his law firm for six months, but that we didn't have any money. His eyes bugged out, and he asked me why he should give us six months of free legal service? I told him that we were offering him a seat on our board. He almost fell off his chair laughing! When he stopped, he said, 'You've got a lot of chutzpah!' and then he accepted my offer. You won't believe what happened next."

"Of course I will," I replied.

"I told him we also needed an accountancy firm on the same arrangement. Could he refer me to one? This time he *did* laugh until he fell off his chair. He called the managing director of a big accountancy firm. He told them, 'I just gave away six months of your services,' and then he laughed himself silly again."

"Good job!" I was impressed, but *not* surprised.

"How're you doing getting the money?" he asked.

"I haven't started yet, but it's a done deal. I still have seven days left."

"How much are you going to raise? I figure we need $50,000," he said.

"One million dollars."

"A million dollars? Are you crazy? Where are you going to get *that* kind of money?"

"Not to worry. It's all taken care of," I said, confidently. I was content to sit on my sofa and wait for the money to show up on my doorstep. Why not? That's how my miracles had come so far.

Russ couldn't sit still. "Let's go out and *get* the money," he suggested. I declined. "Well, let's go sell some ads while we're waiting," he suggested.

"Okay, but on one condition," I answered. "We are not to ask anybody for the million dollars. That's a must." He agreed.

Downtown, we called on banks to see if they wanted to take an ad in our real estate magazine for their mortgage loan department. At the first bank we entered, where we asked to see the president, they showed us directly into his office without an appointment. The president listened intently to my sales pitch, then said that he did not want to take an ad in our magazine because our magazine might offend some of our competitors with whom he did business. "But," he said quickly, "I would like to give you a gift of money to help you get started. What could you use—$50,000? $100,000?"

Russ stared at me in disbelief. I asked what the strings were. The banker said none. I knew he was hoping that once established we would supply him with loan leads garnered by the magazine, but he wasn't requiring it. He asked for a business plan and a proposal for the amount of money we wanted. We said we'd bring these the next day—day 13 of the two weeks I had given God to get me the million dollars.

We rushed to generate our business plan and proposal, working through the night. We had a difficult time knowing how far we could push the envelope on this "free money," but $250,000 was a nice round number. Then we'd only need three more like him and we'd be set. As we left our office, I grabbed a document off the desk on the spur of the moment. At the bank, I handed the president the documents. He closed his eyes, flipped the business plan open to a random page, and put his finger on the page. He opened his eyes and read the fact presented there. "Prove that!" he said.

We hadn't counted on *this*. We had "made up" most of the plan, as is commonly done, but this was a provable fact that he had seized on. Russ and I stared blankly at each other. Then a light bulb came on in my head. The paper I had grabbed, as I was going out the door, was the

45

proof of that particular fact. I pulled it out of my briefcase and pushed it across the desk to him.

He read it, then looked at the proposal. "A quarter of a million dollars?" he screeched. "Are you guys crazy? I'm not giving away that kind of money!"

"Okay, we'll take $100,000," Russ said.

"No, you won't," he cried. "If you need $250,000, then I'd just be throwing my money away, because you'll go bankrupt before becoming a success." And with that, he showed us the door. Russ was deflated, but I wasn't. After all, I reasoned, the million dollars was a done deal. There was probably a reason why we had to go there first.

No other bank showed us into their president's office without an appointment, so we returned to our office to strategize. We tried calling to get appointments, but everybody turned us down. We needed somebody to whom a banker owed a favor to open the door for us. That required us knowing somebody who owed *us* a favor. We called friends until we got one who owed another friend who owed us. The person he referred us to got us the ten-minute appointment with a banker we asked for. "Just tell your buddy that my debt is now paid back," he snapped and hung up in our ear.

The next day, we were shown into the executive vice president's office. "I only gave you guys this appointment because I owed a business acquaintance a favor," he began. "He said you only needed ten minutes." He laid his watch on the desk in front of him and stared at it. "You've got ten minutes . . . go."

I started my sales presentation, but he never took his eyes off his watch. I was watching my own watch, and I stopped talking at nine minutes. Silence. Finally, he looked up and said, "You've still got one minute left."

"That's okay," I replied, "I'm done. Want to buy an ad?"

"No, I don't. But thanks for stopping by anyway," he replied. I got up to head for the door. Russ hesitated. Obviously, he didn't want to give up so soon, but in my mind, a deal was a deal, and we'd had our ten minutes. I called to Russ, and the two of us strode confidently out the door of his office without looking back. Just before the door clicked shut behind us, I heard the banker call out, "Wait a minute!" He said he had one question for us. Did we have a business plan? I gave it to him. He then interrogated us for the next three hours. It was now eight P.M. of the fourteenth day.

The banker reached in his breast pocket and pulled out a checkbook. He wrote in it, tore the check off, and slid it across the desk to us. It was for one million dollars! "I want to buy stock in your enterprise," he said matter-of-factly. Russ gasped. I smiled a knowing little smile. My hand was in my pocket. I was rubbing together my last two nickels in the world as I contemplated the check. "How much stock?"

"80 percent."

"49 percent," I responded. "We want to keep control."

"Not with my money, you don't." he declared.

"When I pick this check up off the table, it won't be your money anymore," I countered, laughing. Fortunately, he and Russ laughed, too.

We negotiated, and the negotiations stretched for weeks, but eventually we took the check and launched our business. Then I did the stupidest thing.

With supreme confidence in my own business prowess, I looked heavenward and said, "Okay, God. Thanks for the money. I can take it from here. You can take a vacation, or whatever. *I'll* run the company." (If that doesn't hit you right between the eyes, it should have. It didn't hit me, until all was lost). My only excuse is that I was new to the miracle business and that was my fatal mistake.

There was a caveat to our operations. We had to launch our business in San Diego. I made arrangements for my children's care, and Russ and I went to San Diego, rented office space, and launched our enterprise.

A Lifetime of Expectation

This lesson reminds me of my friend Joe. Joe had had a challenging childhood, on his own from a very young age. He left home after high school and hit the road as an itinerant musician. He had spent the majority of his life in this manner and developed a sharp edge. Joe is extremely intelligent, with a nimble mind. He never questions his abilities. If he comes upon a problem, he assumes he can fix it, whether he knows anything about the subject or not. He never learned about cars, but if his car ever broke down, and it did frequently, he would grab a wrench and crawl under it, and he wouldn't come out until it was fixed. And it was always fixed. He assumed he could teach himself anything. "Necessity is the mother of invention," he would say. "Oh yeah, and the father of frustration. After all what is more frustrating than need?"

Joe was good at seeing the obvious that escaped everybody else. I got a letter from him one day, and looked for the return address to see where he was mailing it from, since he traveled so much. Written in the upper left-hand corner of the envelope were the words, "Just deliver it!"

I laughed till tears came to my eyes. That was so like Joe. No patience for anybody who couldn't keep up. I knew what he was thinking. "Don't bother looking up here for an excuse to bring this letter back, Mr. Mailman. Just do your job and find Bill."

He was always anticipating what people were going to say, because we are all such creatures of habit. He isn't. The last thing anybody would want to do is challenge Joe. He always topped everybody, and his words could cut through you like a knife. He was exactly right, every time, and witty at the same time, so not only did you lose the argument, you felt the fool besides.

Later in his life, Joe met God. It happened as a miracle. We were driving through the Mojave Desert at a time when he was frustrated with his music career. He was married and had two children, and the strain of constantly traveling to play at clubs and not being able to be with his family was draining him.

I was starting my magazine business and needed good salesmen. Joe could do anything, so I talked him into working for me. He was living in Phoenix at the time, and would need his car for the job, so I volunteered to fly to Phoenix and share the long drive through the Mojave desert to San Diego. He could get settled, start work, then retrieve his family from Phoenix.

As we traveled through the desert, I was on fire to discuss my recent miracles. I explained how I had found God, and the miracles God had wrought. The miles sped by as Joe drove about 70 miles an hour in a 55 mph zone. There weren't any cars on the highway.

All of sudden, a highway patrol car came shooting up out of a sunken dry river bed behind us, lights flashing and siren wailing. "Oh, no," Joe groaned, "I can't afford this! Fifteen over is criminal speeding."

"This is *it!*" I exclaimed excitedly. "Every time I explain God's miracles to someone, God seems to step in and deliver another one. Here's yours, Joe. You are *not* going to get a ticket," I declared.

"Of course, I'm getting a ticket. I was caught red-handed. There's nothing I can say that will make the cop change his mind."

"Joe, listen to me. I know what I'm talking about. Close your eyes, lean your head back on the headrest, and put all of this out of your mind, especially your *worry* and *fatalistic* attitude. Then, just say, 'Father, forgive me for anything I have against anybody. I sincerely forgive them,' and mean it. Then, ask God to make the patrolman not give you a ticket. If you believe what I am telling you, and *believe* that God will deliver this miracle to you, God will."

Joe had been listening to my miracle stories for several hours at this point, and was clearly impressed by them. He looked at me, as if trying to comprehend what I was saying, then shrugged his shoulders. "What have I got to lose? It's all I have left. My back is against the wall." He put his head back, closed his eyes, and made his prayer.

The officer came up to the car window. "Do you know how fast you were going, young man?" he asked politely.

"Yes, sir," Joe replied, "when I heard your siren, I glanced at my speedometer and it read 70 miles an hour."

"That's right, you were 15 over the limit, young man. Let me have your license." Joe handed it to him. The officer went back to his patrol car.

"Hope this isn't an indication of how the rest of the trip is going to go," Joe said.

"Did you finish your prayer?" I asked him.

"Yes, what's next?"

"Nothing. Put it out of your mind. It's a done deal. The ticket isn't going to happen."

"Bill, I was 15 mph over. How can he overlook something like that?"

"Oh, so you think God can't overcome a little challenge like that? If it was going to be easy, Joe, it wouldn't require a miracle."

"Okay, okay, I get it," and he closed his eyes and put his head back again.

"Don't ask again," I admonished. "If you were sincere the first time, don't doubt, it's done. Just sit there, and allow the peaceful feeling of having received a miracle to wash over you," I cautioned.

The officer returned. "Well, I'll tell you what I'm going to do. Since you don't have a bad driving record, I'm going to give you a break and give you another chance. I'm giving you a warning ticket. If you continue to drive recklessly, you will lose your license for sure."

I expected Joe's jaw to drop open, but it didn't. Joe calmly turned and looked at me. "Thanks for the introduction," he said smiling.

I asked the officer, "Do you know of any place here in the desert to get breakfast?"

"Sure do. I was about to go there myself. Just follow me."

When we entered the desert eatery, the place was empty. They seated us and the officer at adjoining tables. We got to chatting, laughing about things with him. When we all got up to go, he grabbed our checks and said, "Breakfast is on me." We just stared in disbelief. During the conversation, I felt Joe wanted to ask him why he had decided to not give him a ticket, but he had the God-given sense not to. I think he realized it wasn't necessary. We both knew Who had helped out in Joe's hour of need.

That was Joe's first encounter with getting a miracle, that he knew of, yet I think Joe, like most of us, could think back to some "lucky" events in his life, and see them for the miracles they are. I've noticed that whenever I tell someone about how God's miracles work, God always seems to step in with a miracle demonstration right then, as if to add veracity to my tale.

Blessings Touch All Lives

When Joe came to work for me, he struggled mightily trying to learn how to ask the right questions to sell properly. He was so used to *telling* everybody what was so obvious to him, it was a hard lesson for him to learn. Of course, I couldn't *tell* him. I could only ask a series of easily answered questions that lead to the self-discovery of the Socratic

Method (see next chapter for explanation). Once he made the breakthrough, he was unstoppable and became my top salesman and eventually, the sales manager.

One day I asked him how he was able to sell the toughest customers.

"Bill, I say out loud, before I go to the door, 'God, let's help these people. Let's get this one for both our sakes.' Then, I just stay with it until they buy."

Joe had learned another secret—when we help others, we help ourselves.

This secret is what makes all our life experiences so rewarding. When we ask for a miracle, such as the million dollars, the other players in the scenario also benefit, even the ones giving the money. Let's return to the story of my million-dollar miracle to see how this lesson unfolded.

7

Actually Getting
What You *Believe*

Everything Falls to Ruin . . .

From the start, Russ and I made mistakes in our business that we'd pay for later. It was thrilling to ride in private jets, stay in penthouses, rent limos, launch a magazine that was a success. In fact, the magazine is still in production now, 21 years later. Virtually overnight, I went from broken in spirit and money to literally flying high. Don't think I didn't know where the credit belonged.

But now *I* was in charge. I didn't have the same self-confidence in my salesmanship skills I once had after so many years away from direct-commission selling. It had been too many years since I had bloodied my knuckles, going door to door as a kid. I hired a sales crew, and one sales manager after another. Each sales manager was worse than the one before and sales were plummeting. Finally, I decided I had to run the sales crew myself. I took over, and sales started to soar. They had gone from an initial $20,000 a month down to zero by the fourth month. When I took over, I retrained my salesmen and sales jumped to $30,000 the first month, and eventually to $90,000 a month. But we kept losing money.

I was working 14-hour days, seven days a week, but we kept sinking financially. My people were doing their best, but something was wrong. I couldn't figure it out all by myself, and I *was all by myself*. After all, God was on vacation. At least, from me. We cut way back in operating and living expenses, moved out of our fancy hotel rooms, and into a cheap, furnished apartment, but still we continued to lose money. The magazine was a success in that the advertisers were making money and the customers were selling their homes. I couldn't figure out what the financial problem was.

One day, Russ came to me for our usual pay-the-bills meeting. By this time, we had opened up a second operation in Milwaukee, Wisconsin. I ran the sales departments and Russ ran the production departments, but we each managed one branch's overall operations. Russ had Milwaukee, and I had San Diego. Our procedure for paying bills was Russ would oversee the bookkeeping, make out the checks, and sign them; then he would bring the bills and the checks to me for review and countersigning before they were mailed. Recently, we had received a blow to the business. Sales were going through the roof with the introduction of a sales telemarketing force, but we had outgrown our rented office space. If we cut back in salesmen to fit the office space, sales would drop to unacceptable levels. We had looked into leaving and moving to larger spaces, but we had a lease on the current space that we couldn't get out of. We considered renting an additional space a few miles away, but splitting the sales crew in half was too hard to work out logistically. We were sunk. It was with heavy hearts that we faced the inevitable. Russ and I agonized over what we could do to resolve the issue, but could think of nothing.

Finally, I went back "upstairs." "Please, God," I prayed, "Help us out of this problem."

While I was reviewing the bills and signing checks that morning, Russ mentioned we had received a phone call the day before from our landlord.

"What did he want?" I asked, half-heartedly.

"He said the company in the space next to ours was moving out. Would we like to consider taking the space next door?"

I was stunned. "And you said what?"

"I told him, no thanks. We can't afford it."

"What? That's the solution to our problem. Our company is saved."

"Bill, it's a separate office. We need one big open space. This is no solution at all."

"We'll ask him to knock out the wall in between."

"He's not going to do that," he said. "Knock out a wall?"

I stared at him in disbelief. "Do you think that God would have gone to all the trouble to 'come' to San Diego, expire the lease of the people *right next door;* then plant the thought in our landlord's mind to call and offer it to *us,* as the perfect solution to the very problem that can cost us our business, and then *not* make the landlord agree to knocking out a little thing like a wall?"

Obviously, Russ and I had a different perception about miracles.

Russ called the landlord. "He said yes!" was his excited reply.

"There was never any doubt in my mind," I said. "*That* was an obvious 'done deal.'"

As clearly as I could see Russ's mistakes, I could see none of my own. Even with the expansion and the increasing sales, production costs continued to scale upward, outpacing our income. The million dollars start-up money was rapidly disappearing. It never once occurred to me to "go upstairs" for a business solution. After all, the business was *my responsibility,* wasn't it?

We had reached nearly the end of our money, when Russ announced he was taking his family on vacation. He asked if I could pick up his production duties. I agreed. I got the idea that maybe we could cheapen the magazine a little without hurting sales by cutting back on the quality of the paper and tightening the layout. I called a meeting with our printer. I told him we had to scale back production costs and asked him for suggestions. He put his pencil to his figures, and then presented me with a new proposal.

He proposed a higher-quality paper and a more spacious layout, but the price was 70 percent less than what we had been paying for our weekly publication. I was incensed.

"How can you afford to do this for this price?" I demanded to know.

He looked sheepish and tried to justify the numbers based on our now large volume. I reminded him that we had been producing at that volume for nearly a year. After some fumbling, the truth came out. He had been overcharging us from day one. In fact, both he and our California printer had been overcharging us.

I demanded a refund. He opened his books to me, as did the other printer when I confronted him as well. Both made a case that if I forced the issue and sued them in court to recover the overpayments, they'd go bankrupt. It would serve them right, I thought, but I knew God did not want me to exact retribution. "Judge not, lest ye be judged" sprang to mind. I forgave them.

Of course, the costs dropped dramatically at once, but it was too little, too late. When Russ got back from vacation, we had to face the fact that we were teetering on bankruptcy. We went to our board of directors for a cash infusion, but that gave our one detractor on the board the excuse he needed to shut us down. He swayed the board, and they refused us. Dejected, we headed back to our office.

The Final Magazine Miracle

I flew to Milwaukee. We contemplated our next and probably final move. "What's our financial status?" I asked Russ.

"We can get this week's magazines out," he said, "but then we'll have to shut down. I'll notify the staffs today that Friday will be their last day of work." That broke my heart.

"And," he continued, "I'll call our landlords and tell them we're bankrupt. It won't be much of a problem here in Milwaukee, because I didn't renew our lease. We've been operating month to month because of that expansion experience in San Diego, but we still owe a few months on our lease in California. All in all, we have a few outstanding creditors. We're probably going to wind up owing $7,500 when we shut our doors that we won't be able to pay. The bills will be dismissed by the bankruptcy court."

"Gee, Russ," I said, "I hate to go out owing anybody any money. After all, they gave us credit in good faith. Isn't there anything we can do?"

"We could take out some home equity loans, but if we fail again, we'll be living at the Rescue Mission."

"I am not willing to gamble the last cent I have in the world and risk my home," I said.

"Why don't you get one of your famous miracles," he said somewhat sarcastically, but with a touch of humor.

Great idea! *That was* what had been missing all this time. I had been trying to perform my *own* "miracles."

"Have we got *any* money left?" I was on fire now.

"$200, if I don't pay any more bills."

"What's the status of our apartment in California?"

"The lease expires next Monday."

"Any airline tickets left?" I had an idea, and was burning hot with it.

"Two round-trip tickets to San Diego."

"Okay, here's the plan. You and I will get on an airplane, fly to San Diego, and use the last of our money to rent a car and buy some meals over the next three days. We'll move into the apartment. That will give us three days to find a buyer for the magazine. After all, it *is* successful and financially sound [now that our printing costs were under control], so, now that we have this last opportunity, we should take advantage of it to get out of debt."

"But tomorrow is Friday. That only gives us the weekend, and there won't be any businesses open on the weekend to buy us out."

"Oh, ye of little faith," I laughed.

We landed in San Diego the next afternoon, rented a car, and drove to our apartment. We got on the phones, and started calling around to see if we could interest a buyer. No "luck." (Actually, to my mind, no miracle that day.) Saturday morning, we dressed for business and met in the living room. We sat on the sofa and stared at each other for a while, then we made small talk. Russ was now pacing the floor.

"Well, what are we going to do, Bill?"

"We're doing it, Russ," I explained. "We're expecting a miracle."

"I can't just sit here and wait. I've got to do something. How about if I drive to our landlord's office and talk about our financial condition and apologize for having to dump the lease?"

"That's fine, Russ. I will be fine just sitting here *expecting* our miracle to walk through that front door, because I *know* that is going to happen. I'll be sitting here, the door will open, and the miracle that we're expecting will walk right through that front door."

Russ left. I busied myself, wrapping up loose ends at the apartment, not giving a care in the world to the dilemma facing us, or the expected miracle. I knew that if I gave it any concern at all, that would be its undoing. We couldn't afford that.

Two hours later, the front door whipped open. Russ flew in, excited. "You'll never in a million years guess what just happened to us!" he shouted.

"Of course, I will," I answered him calmly, smiling, knowing that our miracle had just walked in the front door.

"No! No! Listen!" he was as flustered as I had never seen him. "I was visiting with our landlord, explaining our predicament, when *he* said, 'That's okay about the lease. As it happens, I just had a fellow in here begging to sublease that space until he could lease it direct for himself. Seems it's the perfect location for him. And, oh, by the way, I think I have a buyer for your business.' And, with that, he picks up the phone and calls a client. Did I tell you that he's a certified public accountant? Anyway, he put the client and me on the phone, and we talked, and he will buy the business and give us enough money, up front, to pay off all of our creditors."

I looked up at the ceiling and mouthed a silent "Thank you." "I'm glad it was you who got to bring the miracle in our front door, Russ."

"Oh, yeah . . ." he said reflecting on my "prediction."

We met with the buyer on Sunday and negotiated a fine deal. On the plane ride home I reflected for hours over the past two years and that final weekend searching my soul for lessons learned. It was obvious that it is one thing to understand a concept intellectually, but another to live it in the faith. I had a lot of growing to do . . . spiritually. Once more, I had found myself on the brink of financial disaster. We were able to pay off our debtors and walk away clean, although now there was the matter of earning an income again. . . .

Living the Faith of Miracles

My friend Joe has enormous self-confidence. High school educated, he could have gone on to college, but it didn't interest him. He couldn't wait to go out on his own and start his life. He assumed a few things. He assumed he would be equal to any challenge life would throw at him. He assumed he could figure out the solution to any problem—fixing a car, building musical electronic gear, feeding his family.

Most people I know took a job directly out of school, either high school or college, and got used to a weekly paycheck. Over time, they become dependent on that check, so dependent they fear for their job. "What will happen to me and my family if I lose my job and don't have an income?"

This fear keeps them tied to their job. They humble themselves to the will of others because they cannot imagine life without a paycheck. Over time, in self-disgust at having sold out their principles, they begin to see themselves as diminished human beings. They think they have little or no worth to another employer, so they don't look for another job. Passed over for promotions or raises time after time, they tell themselves that their employer will keep them on because of their loyalty. "After all, haven't I sold myself out time and time again for the good of the company?" People who find themselves in this predicament can become disappointed, angry, defeated, and feel they are unlucky. They dream dreams of the success they might have had. They dream of living in exotic places, and they begin to blame God for having created such an unfulfilled life for them.

Joe never found himself in that position because he never had a job before coming to work for me. That is, he lived life into his forties without ever once having a weekly paycheck. This fact shocked me. I, who had always had a job, couldn't imagine what it was like going from week to week never *knowing* if there would be money for rent, food, gasoline, or whatever. Joe did all the things the rest of us do, got married, had children, bought a house. But he never had a weekly paycheck.

Joe had earned his living as a musician using his God-given natural musical gift playing in bands at nightclubs. He moved from town to town, band to band, as the mood and need struck him. He was cautious with his money because it didn't come in every week, but somehow he was always able to stay afloat doing what he loved.

When I sold the magazine company, I negotiated with the new owner to keep Joe on as vice president of sales. On my last day, Joe and I walked out the front door of the company to shake hands good-bye, as I was departing for the airport to go home.

"I'm leaving, too," he announced.

"Why?" I demanded. "I've just set you up in a high-paying, secure job. Now you won't have to worry about feeding your family."

"I never have," he announced brightly.

"I don't understand."

He told me that before coming to work for me, because of his belief in himself, he *assumed* everything would work out. He didn't see a need to worry about it. "Worry isn't a solution. It isn't even an option. What will worry get you? It not only won't get you anything, it will defeat you."

I grew a lot that day. I was worried about my own future. Where I would go. How I would feed my family when my money ran out and I didn't have a replacement job. The future was unknown, and yet, though I professed a belief in God, I admitted to Joe that I was afraid.

"What is there to be afraid of? If you fear, then you will interfere with your own outlook on life and you will not be where you need to be to find the job you're looking for. More to the point, you won't be in the frame of mind to land the job when you do find it."

He was right. I pondered this concept on the plane ride home. That was 18 years ago, and, while I have had bouts of unemployment since, I am happy to report that Joe was right. None were permanent.

Joe returned to his musical career, his band eventually becoming the most popular group in Phoenix. Then, as if to test his lifelong belief in himself and his belief in an all-providing God, he did what many thought was unthinkable. He said, "This is not Who I Want To Be, Bill. I am not enjoying the nightclub scene. Actually, I never have enjoyed it. It was just the necessary place to be to perform my music. I feel it is not reflective of what my life represents. I have quit playing nightclubs."

"What are you going to do to make a living?" I asked.

"I don't know. I'll play my music, of course. But where? That will be up to God. You *know* that I won't worry about it."

"But aren't all the jobs available at nightclubs?"

"Oh, I sometimes play concerts at sports games. There is work around. Of course, I'll probably take a big dip in income, but the important thing is that I will be living a healthier life, in body, mind, and spirit. It's worth the loss in income to live the life that is important to me."

God came through again and increased his work opportunities in other musical areas and Joe ended up doing better than ever.

Even so, there was one more lesson for Joe to learn, probably the hardest.

"Ego" Gets in the Way

Before Joe learned the lesson of asking questions to find out how he could help his customers, he still had his prowess to defeat any adversary in a verbal exchange. He took pride in it but was frustrated that it was necessary. He was so quick mentally that he was constantly frustrated by people who couldn't keep up, and it galled him to have to backtrack and explain in detail what was so obvious.

Joe felt his life was unfulfilled, so he started going to church. He became an active volunteer playing music for the church services, swinging a hammer when needed, giving church children music lessons. Whatever and whenever something was needed, Joe was ready.

One day, Joe called me, very excited. "Bill, I just had an amazing experience."

"Tell me about it," I replied.

"Well, I had just had an argument with someone, you know, like I always do. I was delivering a devastating blow to this other guy, and I was crushing him under my logic and wit. I remember feeling so superior, having triumphed so devastatingly. Then I came home, but was still troubled over the argument. I felt I was missing something. I lay down, mulling it over. I was remorseful because I had been pretty hard in making my point, again. And as I reflected on the points of the conversation, I kept saying to myself, 'I'm right about this, I know I'm right!'

"And then a strange voice interrupted me, in my own head. An audible voice that calmly said, 'What about kind?' I was convicted to my very soul. 'No,' I said, 'I was not kind, not kind at all.' I am never 'kind.' I felt like a loser at that moment. It is nothing to be smarter than anyone else. All that matters is loving our fellow man, and kindness is how we show that. Oh my god, Bill, what have I been doing all these years? I have been so blind to God's love."

"You've been kind to me," I said weakly.

He laughed. I laughed. We laughed for the longest time. Joe is now working on being kind as often as he (humanly) can. . . .

Why Miracles Are Hard for "Believers"

I'd like to explain how I came to understand how believing in advance works. Believing in advance that we will get our requested miracle at the hour we name only happens when we turn the matter over to God and get out of the way of it ourselves. We can tell God what and when, but not from where or how. Telling God from where and how is taking control, and if we try to keep control, then we have to perform the miracle, and that just isn't going to happen. Telling God what and when is not taking control; it is placing an order, putting God to work. I believe performing miracles is God's full-time job, what He does all day long.

Take faith healing. Believe God will do the healing and God will. But I think it's possible that if someone refuses to go to a doctor, they are telling God not to use doctors to convey miracles. In my opinion, that person is keeping control and determining how God is to work a miracle. I don't think that it's up to us to tell God how to do God's job; just to ask God to do it, and then step back and let God go to work.

Later I relate stories of healing by faith and one potential miracle that failed miserably, and you will see that if God wants to work miracles through doctors, that's okay with me. I believe that it's God's call, God's prerogative. To me, God can deliver my miracles any way God likes, just so long as God comes through. *Belief* to me means *knowing* in advance. If we *know* something is already a done deal, we don't have to dwell on it anymore.

Many of us are God's instrument. Usually we don't even know when God is using or has used us to deliver miracles. Like those ladies who brought food to our door. I doubt that God called them up on the phone and said, "I've got a job for you." I suspect that some urge to perform an act of kindness came over them, and doing what they did made them feel good. Probably, they derived some inner peace, feeling that they were doing the Lord's work. But until they read this book and recognize themselves in it, they'll probably have no idea what their act of kindness for a stranger wrought. There is no finer feeling than knowing that God has used you to perform a miracle in another's life.

Why Miracles Can Be Easier for "Nonbelievers"

I have come to think that we believers mess up because we think that if we believe in God, we should try to help God, and in that we err. Nonbelievers seem to assume sometimes that good things they expect to happen will happen. They don't seem to have any specific reason why they think that. If you pressed them, they would probably say they are "lucky." I believe that when they make that assumption, they are demonstrating faith that God will take care of business for them—even if they don't acredit God with the event or call it a miracle.

Confidence. That's the secret to success. Believing in ourselves. When we feel that we're all alone out there in the world, it's sometimes very hard to maintain blind faith in oneself. There are plenty of detractors telling us how wrong we are. If we believed them, we'd never have any self-confidence, and we'd be doomed.

Depression is losing confidence in ourselves. The antidote is to realize that there is no better, smarter, more correct person on the face of the earth than ourselves. How could there be? How could anyone else know what's best for us? They're not walking around in our skin. They're not facing the challenges that life doles out to us each and every day. Life hasn't given them our friends and our detractors, our challenges and problems. How could they possibly know what's best for us?

What we believe is what we get. If we want to tell ourselves that we're insane, we'll get insanity. If we tell ourselves that we are the brightest, smartest, best-est person in the world, guess what we'll get? Confidence—that's what! When our attitude changes, it shows on our face. It will show in the warm smile we have for everybody we come across, be they a perceived friend or enemy. Our step becomes light. We exude a cheerfulness that others will find captivating. We draw others to us—admirers, really—because we'll be someone they want to be around, someone they want to do good things for . . . so good things start to happen.

Why will they want to do good things for us? Because they'll recognize in us that which they've been searching for all of their lives. They'll see that we have the secret of success and they'll want some. They'll imagine that if they hang around us long enough and stay in our good graces, it will rub off.

Here's an example. A man who thinks he doesn't believe in God goes to college and earns a degree. He assumes this qualifies him for a good job. He goes out into the workaday world and applies at several companies. He gets a couple of interviews, is accepted, and gets the job. What has he assumed? That his credentials got him the job. Is that what happened?

We believe in cause and effect, don't we? It's logical. But consider this: what about the job availability? Is there an element of chance that any job that he was qualified for happened to be available when he graduated and went looking? Luck? What is this mysterious element called "luck"? Is it "chance"? If so, then isn't it possible, even likely, that chance implies good luck or no good luck? By definition, chance isn't always positive, is it? Rather than "chance," is it possible that there is some sort of "organized" pattern to our life?

Take ballerinas and garbage collectors. There are 100,000 garbage collectors born every year for every one ballerina. Thank God! We *need* many, many more garbage collectors than ballerinas for this world to "work." What would happen if, in one year, there were 100,000 ballerinas born for every garbage collector? Would we have garbage collectors dressed in tutus, prancing down our streets collecting our garbage? It seems to me that what appears at first glance to be a chaotic world may have a master plan at work.

So, if we *assume* good luck or *assume* bad luck, what happens? Can we see a correlation? Don't people's expectations usually become self-fulfilling? Know any "Hard Luck Charlies" who seem to always get the bad breaks? Don't they *expect* to not get any "good luck"? What about the young man in our example above? Didn't he go job hunting *expecting* there would be some job available for him at that precise moment?

Everything we expect *is a gift from God; everything is a miracle. God gives us* what we expect. *Every act, done in faith that a particular result will happen,* happens. *If we expect a job to be available, it is. If we expect that it won't be, it won't be. If we expect to have to wait, God grants that* expectation *and* we wait.

The problem nonbelievers face is that when the going gets tough and they lose their confidence in providence or their own positive outlook, without a God, where do they turn for help and understanding? Then the miracles escape them. That is the danger for an atheist or agnostic.

We believers *and* nonbelievers can *control* our destiny. We can cause miracles to happen in our own lives, consciously or unconsciously. The lesson I learned was that the key to having the things, events, miracles we want to happen in our lives, is understanding our relationship to God, and what God requires of us. This was my Aladdin's lamp. We *can* have the *im*probable. We *can* have the *im*plausible. We *can* have the *im*possible. God's power knows no boundaries, no limitations—*only* "expectations." Every religion I have studied confirms what Jesus tells Christians in Mark 11:22–25: Believe in God and *all* things are possible.

I can tell you from experience not only that they are possible, but that what you believe—truly believe in your heart—*will* happen, no matter how illogical.

8

Fear Undoes Miracles

Rising from the Ashes

As I contemplated what I wanted to do next, I went over the successes we had had with the magazine operations in my mind. I *really* enjoyed training the salesmen. I delighted in their successes. I liked taking them out, having them watch a sale come together, watching them sweat trying to close a sale, and then getting it.

My training approach was based on two concepts I had come to appreciate over my career. The first was the principle that we really can't sell anybody *anything* . . . especially if they don't want to buy it . . . presuming that they didn't want to buy my product because it was not right for them in solving a business problem they had. The second was that we can't *sell* anybody anything, we can only facilitate their own decision to *buy*.

1. Afraid to Buy

That's the only reason products and services exist—to serve a need. I have found that people can also be fearful, even when it comes to buying a product that they really want and need. The concept of "buying" anything often is scary for most people. Nobody wants to make a mistake, and yet they have to make decisions based on limited information and on believing the salesman's word. Very few people are willing to trust a salesman. After all, it's his job to sell us something, anything, so he can earn his living.

So I had to raise my salesmen's perceptions that I didn't want them selling anything to just anybody. I needed them to see that the only way they could sell consistently was to be a sales facilitator: Find out what the customer's needs are, analyze whether our product is the best solution at the right price, and only then close the sale.

2. *The Socratic Method*

The second step was to *train* them in how to discover the customer's needs, to see if they could help them. This isn't easy because fearful customers tend not to open up with salesmen, lest they accidentally buy something they didn't intend. Socrates figured out the solution to this some 3,000 years ago, and so did the TV lawyer Perry Mason. I am a big fan of the "Perry Mason method" of problem solving. Perry Mason always got his criminal to confess on the witness stand by asking him questions that led him down the path to the ultimate truth. Even if one tried to lie, Mason asked the right series of questions from which there was no escape. This is the ultimate application of The Socratic Method.

Socrates argued that his method was a process of asking a series of easily answered questions, the truthful conclusion of which has been foreseen by the questioner, that lead the answerer to the inevitable, universal truth. Mason had to know who the guilty party was and how they did the crime in advance, so that he would know which questions to ask that would lead the criminal to the inescapable truth of the crime.

The theory is a sound one, and can be applied in all walks of life. The successful parents draw their children out, while building their self-confidence as they help the children problem-solve for themselves. A boss can use it to help his employees learn and salesmen can use it to help their customers solve their own problems. The key is that if only open-ended, honest questions are asked, there is no other place to arrive than at the truth of a situation.

Consider this: From birth onward, we learn by being *told* everything others want us to learn (parents, teachers, friends). So, what do we learn to do? Since children learn what they live, *not* what they're told, they learn to *tell*. What we should be learning is to *ask questions*. Salesmen who *tell* their customers what to buy fail regularly. That's why direct commission salesmen only close 20 percent of their potential sales. But a good Socratic salesman only asks questions and never tells his customer anything. Similarly, instead of telling God *how* to perform miracles, maybe just asking for a miracle is best.

A New Career

So, I was back home, thinking over all this on my best thinking place, my sofa, staring out the window again. God and I hadn't talked for a long time. Of course, I was used to it being a one-way conversation because God never "spoke" to me. But the silence was profound: God's a great listener and very sympathetic. I had never seen a job advertised as "sales trainer," but that's what I wanted to do. "Oh, well, let's go for it, Big Guy."

I took out the "Help Wanted" section of the newspaper, and dropped it on the floor to the Ss. I looked at the columns. There was an ad for a sales trainer for the *Suburban Yellow Pages*. I called for an interview and was told to come at seven P.M.

When I showed up, there was a line of 35 people and I was at the end of it. More got in line after me. When it came my turn, the interviewer was burned out, having repeated the same "bait and switch" message over and over. It seemed nobody wanted to be a commissioned salesman, but everybody wanted to be a sales trainer on the assumption that it was a fixed salaried position. The interviewer went into his routine saying that before someone could actually *be* the sales trainer, they had to *first* be a commissioned salesman for the company.

I asked him what his job title was. "Sales trainer," he said. It was obvious the job I was looking for wasn't "open." I asked for the phone number of his boss. I called and made an appointment for a telephone conference. Friday at ten A.M. I was standing in his outer office. He was surprised and not pleased to see me there, but he allowed me a ten-minute interview. I came out an hour later with the advertised job. The deal we struck was that, since his annual sales had been flat at $1 million for the past several years, I promised to double his sales within the next 12 months; if I came even $1 short of that, he didn't owe me anything. If I achieved that goal, however, he owed me $50,000. He agreed to pay me in monthly increments for each month that sales at least doubled.

I trained their salesmen using my two principles, and I went out with them into the field on sales calls. Sales doubled to $2 million by the ninth month.

That was good, but then I was out of a job again.

What followed was a series of other sales trainer jobs on the same basis. I wish I could report that everything was miraculous after that, but I cannot. I discovered that I was just as human as ever, given to the same fears and foibles as my fellows. The road was rocky. Up and down went my opportunities and finances. But during the next 14 years, God and I communed regularly. God helped me out, from time to time, as I was able to keep a proper perspective on our relationship—and keep the faith. That wasn't easy. In fact, sometimes it was impossible. I didn't get down on myself at those times. I knew whose fault it was. Of my fallibility, there was no doubt.

The miracles I requested properly (always fulfilled) were sporadic. The lesson was that no matter how good my intentions, if I failed to believe *in advance* that the miracle would happen—had already happened in the future—or if I *worried* about the outcome, I never got those miracles.

The rule about miracles is faith *first, then* proof. If God were to rip the roof off your house right now and stick a gigantic face down in place of your ceiling and say, "Here I Am!" well, we'd *all* be on our knees. But God doesn't work that way. *First,* we must *believe.* Only *then* do we get "proof" by way of miracles.

The Home Buyers

During this period, I took a job as the manager of a real estate office. While I have a real estate broker's license, I had never sold a house. My experience as a sales manager and sales trainer qualified me to manage the agents. We kept long hours, because much of real estate is sold in the evenings. I was always the first one in office in the morning and the last one out at night, which made for some long days.

I would wait until all of my agents were back from their evening showings, in case they had an offer-to-purchase to write. I had to review the contracts and didn't want to hold up a deal by making them wait for the next business day. If I had an agent out with clients past nine P.M., I would leave the lights on but lock the door, then let the agent and clients in when they arrived. One evening, I forgot to lock the door. About ten P.M., a couple in their thirties with two children entered the office.

"I'm sorry," I said, "but we're closed."

"Well, the lights are on, the door is open, and you're here, aren't you?" the woman said sweetly.

"Yes, well," I stammered, "but you see, I'm the manager and I'm just waiting for one of my agents to check in."

"Well, we need to buy a home tonight, so you will have to help us," she declared.

"Why tonight?"

"Because we want to move in tomorrow morning," she said. I was incredulous. Nobody could be this uninformed.

"Ma'am," I said, "That's impossible. First, we have to find you a suitable home you can afford, submit an offer-to-purchase, wait for the counter-offer, then negotiate. Then you have to apply for a mortgage and the house has to be appraised. There is no way you could move into a house, even if we could find you one tonight, in less than six weeks."

"Oh, it won't be any problem at all."

"Why is that?" I asked, expecting her to tell me they were going to pay cash for the house, which would expedite the process.

"Because I asked God to give us a home by morning and He never lets me down."

"Well, even if I had an agent available, it's way too late tonight to find you a home," I declared.

"You're licensed, aren't you?" she asked.

"Well, yes, but I've never sold a home and am not expert enough for you to trust," I demurred.

"Well, you *must* believe in God, don't you?!" she persisted.

"*Of course, I do*," I proclaimed, indignantly. "On *that* issue, there is no question."

"Do you believe in miracles?"

"Absolutely. I've had many."

"Look. I prayed and asked God to get me a home we could move into by morning because we have nowhere to live. We had made arrangements to buy a house on a land contract from an older woman in the city. She was to finance it for us. We live up north about 200 miles, and my husband just got a job here last week. We moved into her home, but she didn't move her things out. When I asked her when she planned to move, she said she had no intention of moving. She just wanted a family to live with her.

"We told her this wasn't our understanding and she had to leave. Well, she wouldn't, and we were relegated to the basement. All four of us. We have been washing in the gas station restroom and we can't go on like this, all huddled together in a basement. That's when I decided to ask God for a miracle tonight. I bundled the family into our car and started driving around looking for a Realtor. And here you are: God's miracle Realtor. Surely you are not going to deny God?"

I looked past them out into the parking lot and saw their wreck of a car. "How much money do you have?"

"We don't have any money at all. My husband has been an alcoholic for the past ten years and unable to work steadily. I've kept the family going working part time as a waitress."

My eyes popped out of my head. How could she possibly think they could buy a home, overnight, with no money at all?

"Why didn't you work full-time?"

"I couldn't," she answered, "because I had to give the other hours of the week in volunteer service to the Church."

"That couldn't have left you much money to live on."

"We get by, with God's help, and we're not picky. We'll take the cheapest house on the market."

"Okay, okay," I surrendered in disbelief. After all, who was I to interfere with her miracle. I got out my listings book and turned to the first page, because listings start at the lowest priced ones, and looked for the least expensive house. I found one for $54,000.

"How much does your husband make?" I asked her, because he had been sitting there mute, not joining the conversation.

"Well, he was lucky to get anyone to hire him with his poor work history and being a recovering alcoholic. He's a janitor at Harnischfeger and makes $6 an hour."

"That's less than $12,500 a year," I said. "The most you can afford is a $36,000 house and there aren't any, and that's presuming a bank would take the chance without a down payment. Most unlikely!"

"And *you* claim to believe in miracles," she demanded.

"Okay, okay," I said. I called the listing Realtor at her home and made the verbal offer. At first, she was thrilled to have anyone show an interest in this "lemon" of a house that had sat on the market for over a year, that is, until she heard the offer. Then she was indignant. I insisted she call her owner and present our offer. She called back in a few minutes with a counter-offer of $45,000. "What you don't understand about these buyers," I stressed, "is that they have *no* money, and they earn no money to speak of. They'll be lucky to find a bank to go along with their $36,000 offer!"

"My owner won't accept that," the Realtor said.

"You don't have the right to speak for your owner," I replied. "You *have* to present our counter-counter-offer."

She got back to me in a few minutes. "I will meet you at the home at eight A.M. sharp. And when they see this little jewel of a house, they'll meet our price."

My client marched confidently out of my office at eleven P.M. singing, "See you in the morning."

I dreaded what this house was going to look like. After all, it was the cheapest house on the market and in the worst part of the city. The next morning at eight A.M. I met the family and the Realtor. She swung the fence gate open, and I caught my breath! The house was adorable. It was a cute Cape Cod style house, complete with dormers and new carpeting throughout. The woodwork had been stripped and restained, including all the doors, windows, and arches. A new linoleum floor had been laid in the kitchen, overshadowed by a new refrigerator, oven, range, and cabinets. The children delighted in the upstairs rooms, which featured twin beds and built-in shelves and desks, all freshly painted in white enamel. The house was indeed a jewel.

"We'll take it," my client said.

"Then we'll drive over to the home of the owner, and conclude the negotiations," the Realtor said and marched back to her car.

We drove out to the suburbs and pulled up in front of a huge ranch home that must have been worth $250,000. We were met at the front door by a bear of an old man, dressed in overalls. He had working man's hands but a pleasant, quiet demeanor. He led us into the kitchen, where we sat down at the table as his wife poured us coffee and put out rolls.

"What's the matter with you, mister?" the owner challenged my client's husband. "Why aren't you willing to provide at least the minimum basic house for your family at a reasonable price?"

I stared in disbelief at the other Realtor as she allowed this conversation to take place. Realtors *never* let the customers talk to each other directly. It's like with lawyers: Your representative does all the negotiating to keep control of the sale. But she seemed perfectly willing to let the owner talk directly to my client, so who was I to question it?

"Well, sir," the husband stammered, "I am willing. My Realtor says I just can't afford any more—you see, sir, I am a recovering alcoholic. I've been unemployed for ten years and just last week got a job as a janitor over at the Harnischfeger plant."

"Harnischfeger!" the owner said. "Who do you work for?"

"A nice gentleman by the name of Charley Rogers," he answered.

"You can have the house for your $36,000," the owner announced.

"Excuse me," I interrupted. "We're not sure we can find a bank that'll make the loan just yet."

"No problem," the owner replied. "I'll finance it myself, on a land contract."

"But you don't even know if this guy's good for it," the owner's agent protested. "He hasn't even been qualified."

"Look," the owner replied, "I just retired after 36 years as head of Harnischfeger's maintenance department. Charley Rogers came to me as a reformed alcoholic 15 years ago. I took a chance on him and he worked out just fine. If this guy's good enough for Charley, he's good enough for me! I'm giving him the house for his price, right here and now!"

"Sir," I interjected. "If you don't mind my asking, why is the house in such brand-new condition?"

"Son," he said to me, "my father built that home. I grew up in that home. And I raised my family there. I lived in that home my entire life. We just bought this place last year for our only son, who has Down syndrome. I couldn't leave the homestead rundown. I had to fix it up for some deserving young family, like your people here, who will take loving care of it."

My clients were beaming, tears rolling down their cheeks—in fact, mine and the Realtor's, too.

"Can we move in this morning?" the woman asked.

The owner reached into his pocket and pulled out a set of keys. He threw them down on the table to the husband. "Be my guest!"

It was nine A.M. and as the woman had predicted, here they were, moving into their new home. God sure moves quickly when God wants to.

As we turned to part, my client turned to me and asked, "Did you ever doubt God, Mr. Tucker?"

"Absolutely *never!*" I replied, but I have to admit, I walked to my car lightheaded and lightfooted, as if walking on air.

9

Living Miraculously

Back to the Mall Business

When these sales training assignments ran out, I went "Upstairs" again.

I was standing in the lobby of my last employer, having been summarily dismissed after doubling their sales. I was staring out the window wondering what I was to do next, since I had run out of direct commission sales customers. My eyes suddenly focused on what was visible out that window. It was the classiest shopping center in town. I had managed the two largest malls, but here was the most elegant and reputable mall staring me in the face. "I could go back into the mall business at Mayfair Mall," I reasoned with myself, "for a respite and safe harbor to rebuild my finances."

Looking heavenward, I said, "Okay, God, here's the deal. I want to be the manager of that shopping center across the street and I want that job within the next 30 days! But I don't want anybody to have to lose their job to make an opening for me." Then I said, "Thank you," because I knew it was a done deal. I put the matter out of my head so I wouldn't be tempted to worry about it.

Almost four weeks later I was required to visit our local banker to complete tax forms for our magazine business that Russ and I had licensed to the California publisher. While sitting at his desk, the banker asked me if I intended to apply for the mall manager's job at Mayfair. I was shocked. "Why?"

He replied, "They advertised last week for a mall manager and I thought at the time, who better qualified than you. Since you're currently out of work . . ." he said, not finishing his sentence. I just smiled a knowing little smile. After all, the 30 days was just about up.

I called the mall. The secretary who answered said, "I'm sorry, but applications are now closed."

"That's okay," I replied, "Just tell the boss that I am on the phone and he will open them up again."

"No, he won't," she said adamantly.

"Just please give him my name," I implored her. She said it was a waste of time, but she would do as I asked. She came back in a moment and scheduled an interview for me.

I always wear my best business suit whenever I have an interview, but as I contemplated my choice that morning, I laughed and selected my most unimpressive suit. After all, it couldn't possibly adversely affect the outcome. The outcome was a done deal.

When I showed up for the appointment, the vice president invited me to sit down next to him at the table, and he explained that, heretofore, the mall had never had a manager. He had been running the day-to-day operations, but it had become such a big job, he decided several weeks ago to create a mall manager position. (All was going according to plan.) He talked nonstop for the next two hours, rarely asking me any questions. I was a good listener. I had learned through sales that it is the good listener, not the talker, who gets the sale.

Finally, he said, "I don't know why I am doing this, because you are the weakest candidate from my field of 16 qualified applicants, but I am now offering you the job. Would you like to start Monday?"

Monday was the 30th day. I accepted.

Angels Also Deliver Miracles

Some people believe in angels. Could God use angels to deliver miracles? I guess that's a rhetorical question. Is there anything God *can't* do? Miracles can be for big things, great things, wonderful things, but they can also be for little things. Here's an example.

I was living in the Midwest far north. It was winter. I had to travel to a tiny town for a banquet honoring local children I had responsibility for through my volunteer organization. The roads were clear when I left home for the 30-mile drive.

That night, when we were leaving the restaurant where the banquet had been held, I discovered that snow had been falling for hours and was a foot deep. I got in my car to start it up only to discover that my battery was dead. I had my headlights on during the daylight for safe driving and hadn't turned them off. I hurried back to the restaurant, hoping to find somebody to help me. Everyone was gone, the restaurant was dark, and no one answered my knock. The entire town was dark. Apparently, everybody had already gone to bed. Not wanting to disturb anyone, I looked for a gas station.

Fortunately, the one on the next corner was one for which I had a service club membership, but it was closed. A sign on the window gave the phone number of the owner, in case of emergencies. I called it, and the owner's wife answered.

"I'm sorry," she said, "but the station is closed now."

"I understand," I pleaded, "but I'm desperate. My battery's dead and I'm 30 miles from home and you don't have a hotel in this town. Couldn't your husband please come out and give me a jump start?"

"I'm sorry," she continued, "but Sam's out in the back 40 rounding up the cattle because this is going to be one lollapalooza of a storm."

"Please," I implored her, "or, if not, can you refer me to another station? I belong to your auto club."

"Oh, the auto club?" she perked up, "That won't be a problem then. Sam will be out as soon as he gets the cattle in."

Two hours later, Sam jump-started my car. I thanked him and started on my way out of town, dreading the drive over the twisting, two-lane highway at the posted speed limit of 35 miles per hour. I got about 300 yards out of town as large snowflake flurries rushed at my windshield, restricting my view to about 20 feet. There were no streetlights out in the country, so I only had my headlights, which had to be on low beam. The blanket of snow reduced the landscape to a sea of smooth white. There was no way to tell where the ditch was on either side of the road.

I had a yardstick in the back seat, so I decided to get out of the car and walk ahead, probing the snow for the edge of the road. I walked 30 feet and stuck the stick in the snow at the road's edge. Then I got back in my car and inched it forward to the stick. Then I got out, and repeated the procedure. I kept this up for an hour, but had only moved forward another 300 yards. The snow kept coming down.

I realized that, at this pace, I might get home sometime in late spring. If I survived. Oh my god, I might *not* survive. If I tried to just wait out the storm until morning, my car would run out of gas and I could freeze to death before help could arrive. "I'd better walk back to town and wake someone up who could give me shelter for the night."

I got out of my car and looked back. The town was not visible. No lights. The road behind me was completely covered with snow. I couldn't even retrace my tire tracks. I wasn't even sure of the way to walk back because the road had been twisting so much in the last 300 yards. Moreover, if I tried to turn my car around on the tiny road, I could slip off into the ditch. I was stuck.

I got back in my car to consider other solutions. None presented themselves. I'm a dead man, I thought.

I remembered God. I prayed. "Please, God, help me. I am lost and alone, except for You. Please help me out of this storm and back home to my family. And, please forgive me, for aught I have against any." I had *no* doubt that God would answer my prayer.

Just then, a *whoosh* swept past my car. I saw the strange taillights of a car receding out of sight in front of me. The car must have been traveling the speed limit. By the time what had just happened registered with me and I had collected my wits, the car was a good 300 feet ahead of me and disappearing fast.

I can follow him, I thought. I pressed down the gas pedal and sped off after him. As he made a swerve on the road, I made a mental note of exactly how far in front of me that curve was, and turned there, where I thought he had turned. The snow was coming so fast and furious, I couldn't see well enough to follow his tire tracks, so estimating the distance was all I had to go on.

I maintained the 100 yards distance between us. I marveled at how fast he was driving. Surely he couldn't see the road any better than I. He must have every turn in this road memorized, I reasoned to myself. Further, I tried to identify the model car it was, because the taillights were none that I had ever remembered seeing before. His taillights were all I could see. It was ethereal. I couldn't see any other part of the car in the dark and the flurries, just the taillights.

We traveled on this way, my anonymous friend and I, for close to an hour. As we neared the city where I lived, I recognized that over the next rise, the road became a four-lane highway, and was well lit and straight as an arrow for the final five miles into the city. I'm safe, I exulted. I saw the driver shoot up over the rise and disappear down the other side. I increased my speed to narrow the gap. I've got to catch up with him and thank him for saving my life, I thought.

By the time I shot up over the rise, I couldn't have been more than a block behind him. As my car burst onto the lighted, straight stretch, the flurries had subsided, and I could see for five miles ahead of me. The car was nowhere to be seen! He couldn't have turned off anywhere, I reasoned, because there were no crossroads for miles ahead. I pushed my gas pedal to the floor. I was overwhelmed with appreciation and I *had* to thank him.

He was nowhere to be seen. As I slowed down for the last couple of miles to my home and the waiting arms of my family, I reflected on what this apparition could have been. It occurred to me it must have been an angel sent by God in answer to my prayer. I could think of no other explanation.

Later I saw the evolution of that miracle. The key was the yardstick. Why did I have a yardstick in the backseat in the first place? I would never have a reason to have a yardstick in my car and never did have one there. Yet I had been given this yardstick a few days earlier by a hardware store clerk as a promotion. I had unthinkingly tossed it on the backseat.

When I was at the point in my journey home where I could have turned around and sought refuge in the town, the presence of the yardstick encouraged me to use it to go further on, thereby sealing my fate, putting myself out there too far from the town to turn back. Had God seen to it that I got the free yardstick so that I would *have* to rely on an angel and learn another lesson about my relationship with God?

Our "need" in life is to see all events as either miracles or the steps that lead to what we call "miracles" (great beneficences from God).

Therefore, I reason, when "bad" things happen in my life, they are not really bad things at all. They are the stepping-stones to a miracle. They are the steps that lead to our miracles. And miracles are our steps to finding God proactive in our lives.

10

Everyone Can Have Miracles

The Hollywood Trip

One time my parents won a free trip to Hollywood. My family was of modest means, so the folks didn't get to travel much in their lifetime. When my mother won a free trip to Hollywood so that she and my father could be the guests of a television production company, the prospect of being in the studio audience and going backstage afterwards to meet the "stars" was a dream come true.

The big day for their flight to California finally arrived. Mom and Dad were looking forward to escaping winter and basking in the California sunshine. Mom insisted we get to the airport by ten A.M., even though their flight wasn't until one P.M. She was taking no chances on missing it. The deal was they make this flight or the trip was forfeited.

When we arrived at the airport, it was packed with thousands of holiday travelers. The lines were 50-people long at each reservation counter, and there were at least 50 such counters. I had my parents take seats while I stood in line for them. A blizzard raged outside. So far, the early morning flights had still taken off and without incident. Then came the devastating announcement. All flights were postponed while the airport de-iced airplanes and plowed snow from the runways. Soon flights started to be canceled. Passengers rushed from airline to airline, searching for seats on a later flight.

Then even those flights were canceled. People started to drift out of the terminal as their last hopes dried up. We sat on the bench seats facing the airline counters, my parents worrying. "Don't worry, you'll make it out," I said. I had every confidence God would come through.

As the day wore into early evening, the airport was emptying out. Every time I approached the counter, the agents said they still had hopes the storm would abate, they'd get the runways cleared, and the planes would start flying again. So we waited. And waited. And waited. Eventually all flights were canceled.

"Well, I guess the trip was not meant to be," my father said resignedly.

"Don't give up the faith, Dad," I replied. "Somehow, some way, God is going to deliver you an airplane and you'll make the trip yet."

I approached the counter and asked if there were any flights originating elsewhere that were scheduled to make a stop in Milwaukee, continuing on west.

The agent said that there was one flight left at ten P.M. leaving Detroit, scheduled to stop in Milwaukee and continue to Los Angeles. "But even though the storm has stopped in Detroit, it's still coming down too heavy here," she said.

I asked what that meant. She said that if the plane couldn't put down in Milwaukee, it would just fly over without stopping.

At five minutes to ten P.M., the agent rushed over to us. "The clouds have broken!" she declared excitedly. "The plane is landing to pick your parents up." I looked around the empty expanse of the airport. We were the only ones left in the whole place. My father looked at me, and said, "I guess they, too, should have kept the faith."

Little Miracles

Much later in life, after my father was gone and my means were again modest, my mother was living on her social security. This miracle illustrates teaching others to find their miracles.

My mother had an unexpected expense to her car, so she had saved her pennies until she had the $80 she needed. The day she finally had accumulated that amount, I arranged to meet her with my son for dinner. We parked next to each other in the restaurant's parking lot.

When we came out of the restaurant, we noticed my mother's car door was ajar. "Oh, no!" she cried. We rushed over to her car to discover it had been broken into. The burglar's tools were lying on the driver's seat.

"My money!" my mother shrieked. She rifled her glove compartment, and then broke down sobbing, "My $80 is gone!" She had put the cash in the glove compartment in anticipation of taking her car to the garage the next morning. I felt bad because I did not have $80 to give her. I refrained from lecturing my mother about the foolishness of leaving cash in her car because that would be of no use other than to make her feel worse and she had obviously learned that lesson the hard way.

We called the police, and the officer who arrived searched her car thoroughly. "I put the cash right on top of that stack of papers in the glove compartment," my mother said. The officer meticulously took each piece of paper out of the glove compartment and looked at it scrupulously before putting it back to make sure the money was actually gone. "I'm sorry, ma'am," he said, "but I'm afraid that your money is gone, and you never can count on getting your cash back even if we do find the thief, which is doubtful."

It was only $80, but to my mother it was a devastating loss. "Bill, what am I going to do?"

"Pray and ask God to return your cash, Mom, and believe in advance that He will," was all I could say. I believed that admonition to the core of my soul. I knew if she did, God would provide.

That night she tossed and turned all night unable to sleep for the worry over her loss. She fell asleep eventually. When she awoke, she reflected on my words of the night before and decided to ask God to return her money. After saying her prayer, she felt a calm come over her and she relaxed. A few moments later, she felt an urge to check her glove compartment. There was the $80 in cash sitting on top of the stack of papers.

The Innocence of Children's Faith

When my son was five, I took him to Disney World in response to his pleadings, but I made it a surprise. I told him we were going on a surprise trip, but not where. I drove to the airport and we boarded the plane for Florida. His look of amazement at the vastness of the airport and then as he looked out the plane's window as we took off was a delight. This must be the sort of pleasure God enjoys when we ask God for a miracle and God provides it (because we believe in advance that God will). God must delight in seeing the awe and the glee in our faces at that moment, or the tears of joy, if that is how we meet our miracle blessings.

When we arrived, there was a light misty rain that persisted the whole day. We wore rain slickers, but wished for a sunny experience on our holiday. The second day as we sat at the hotel's shuttlebus stop to Disney World, my son looked at me with trusting eyes, eyes of belief in the God-like powers of a parent, and asked, "Daddy, can you make the rain stop?"

A couple of adults nearby chuckled at the innocence of the question. "No, son," I said. "But God can if we believe He will, but we both have to believe very much."

"Oh, I believe He will, Daddy!" he exclaimed. The adults frowned. I imagined that they were thinking what a terrible parent I must be to mislead my child with such foolishness.

"Okay, Matt," I said, "Here's what we must do. We must pray and ask God to stop the rain in one minute. Then we will count down 60 seconds by counting one-thousand-one, one-thousand-two, and so on, okay?"

Beaming, my son looked up at me with total belief for he had no reason to doubt me. When I saw that affirmation in his eyes, I could not disbelieve myself. I knew God was about to reward such faith.

We started to count. When we reached one-thousand-sixty, the rain abruptly stopped, and the sun broke through the clouds. The smile on my son's face had been there the entire time we were counting. It wasn't as if he was waiting to see if it would happen. He knew it was about to happen and was enjoying the anticipation. The other adults looked at us as if we were possessed and scootched a little further away from us down the bench. Obviously, they didn't understand what they were seeing.

I laugh about it now because it was probably one of the worst miracles we ever asked for, because in July, when the sun comes out in Florida, the heat is insufferable. We sweltered for the next three days. It didn't occur to us to ask God to return the misty rain.

The Miscarriage

In my job as the sales trainer for the Suburban Yellow Pages, I relearned a lesson in faith that I had known instinctively years before, but it had not jelled in my mind. Until a very young woman taught it to me.

My telemarketing department supervisor came into my office one morning and said, "Susan didn't come into work today."

"Why? What's the problem?" I inquired.

"She had a miscarriage last night," was his reply.

"Oh, I am so sorry to hear that. Well, give her a few days to recuperate. In fact, let her have a week. But I want her back here a week from today."

"Maybe she'll need longer than that," he said pensively.

"Maybe she will, and that'll be okay, *if* she has a medical reason," I said, "but for every day after one week, I want a medical explanation. You see, Bob, a major loss like this can be devastating to one's emotional stability and work is a good antidote. If she is depressed over the loss, getting her mind back on work and off herself will be good medicine."

"Okay," he said. I appreciated his managerial skills and his caring attitude about his employees. He respected others and showed it, so he had excellent rapport with and loyalty from his people. We had a natural, easy relationship, and I admired him greatly. He was back the following Monday morning to report that Susan would not be back that day.

"Why? Is there a physical problem?"

"Noooo." He was hesitant. "She felt she wanted more time off. It seems that this is not her first miscarriage and her husband is so disappointed he's blaming her."

"That concerns me," I said. "If she refuses to come in tomorrow, please tell her that I'd like to take her to lunch." It was my intention to talk to her about God, to see if I couldn't help her heal. Besides, I wanted to explain how wrong her husband was for blaming her, to give her some balance.

The next day, she again decided not to come in to work, but Bob had made a lunch appointment for us at a nearby restaurant. I was taken aback by her cheerful demeanor. "You know, Susan," I started, "we really miss you at work. You are one of our very best workers and the place isn't the same without you."

"I'm sorry, Mr. Tucker," she responded, "but I needed some time to myself."

"Well, that's perfectly all right," I replied, "but, you know, it might be helpful for your recovery to busy yourself with work. May I tell you a little story about God and why this unfortunate event may have happened to you?"

She reached her hand across the table and touched mine, much as a parent wanting to soothe a child might do. "Oh, that isn't necessary," she said, "I know all about God. I can tell you are worried about me, but let me put your mind at ease. I am not depressed and I am not blaming myself for the miscarriage. True, I am very saddened by it, and it isn't my first. But I know that God has His reasons, and I'm okay with it."

My shock at this wisdom must have shown on my face.

"May I tell *you* a little story, Mr. Tucker?"

"I would be delighted," I said, relaxed now and smiling.

"When I was a young teenager, my best friend was from a very wealthy family, while my father was working class. My friend's parents took every summer off and traveled the world. They of course took their daughter with them on these three-month excursions. We were very sad because we always hoped to spend our summers together.

"One such summer, my friend said she was going to ask her father if she could not go on the trip and spend the summer at our house, if that would be okay with my family. My parents said that would be no problem. But when she asked her father, he said, 'Let's take Susan with us to Europe, all expenses paid.' We were so excited. I rushed home to tell my parents. 'Absolutely *not!*' my father bellowed.

"I was surprised. I couldn't believe my ears. Why would he deny me this wonderful opportunity? I burst out crying and ran to my room. I overheard my father explain to my mother. 'This family doesn't take charity from anyone. If my daughter wants to go to Europe, it's my responsibility to pay for it for her. We're not taking any handouts!'

"It wasn't about Europe, Mr. Tucker. It was about us being together, my friend and I. I was still lying on my bed crying, when my grand-mother came over for a visit. She came into my room and asked me what was the matter. When I explained, she said, 'Oh, dear, I can fix that.'

"'How?' I wanted to know. Grandma said, 'All you have to do is pray and ask God to change your father's mind and God will!' she declared cheerily. So I did. I got down on my knees next to the bed and prayed very hard for my father to relent and let me go.

"Then I jumped up, and ran into the living room, and asked my father if he had changed his mind? 'No,' was his response, 'and if you ask again, I'll ground you for the summer!' Again, I was devastated, and burst out crying again and ran back to my bedroom.

"Grandma said she couldn't understand it. She said it always worked for her. Then she asked me, 'Dear, let's review this. First you knelt and prayed and asked God to change your father's mind, right?' I said yes. 'and then you said, thank You, right?'

"'No, I didn't say thank You,' I told her. Why would I? God hadn't done it yet.

"'Oh, dear, you *must* say thank You so that God knows that you understand that God has *already* granted your wish. You see, God can only give you a miracle if you know that God already has.'

"Well, Mr. Tucker, I got back down on my knees and prayed again, and this time when I finished my prayer, I said thank You. At that moment, I felt like a great weight was lifted from my shoulders. I was at peace. I knew that I didn't have to rush out and *see* if father had changed his mind. Somehow, I just *knew* in my heart that it would all work out, some way. At that moment, my bedroom door opened and my father came in and said that he had changed his mind. I could go. I never forgot that lesson."

I got chills over that beautiful story. I thanked her for sharing. She thanked me for my understanding. She came back to work the next day.

Depression

One night around eleven P.M., I got a phone call from an old Navy buddy. "Bill, I need your help. I'm only a few blocks away from your home. May I stop over?"

I assured him that he could. A few minutes later he arrived at my door. I was really surprised, because it wasn't like "Germ" to call so late so unexpectedly, as he lived 200 miles north.

After we got settled down in our chairs, Germ explained the reason for his unexpected late-night visit. He had a friend who lived in the neighborhood next to my subdivision. His friend was depressed, and Germ wondered if I would go over to the man's house and help his friend out of his depression.

I said I would be glad to, but I wasn't sure there was anything I could do. Germ was worried about his friend. His wife of 28 years had left him and he had lost his job, too. He just sat at home staring out the window. He had gone through all his money. Germ was concerned that he wasn't taking any action to solve his problems.

"He has sunk far lower since then," said Germ, "and I'm afraid he's suicidal. Might even be tonight. He's about to lose his home, and I think that is pushing him over the edge. His career is over, his children are grown, and his wife is gone. He feels he has no reason to go on living. I don't know what I can say that will snap him out of it. Then I thought of you. You've been through this and you made it back, so I thought maybe you could help."

I said again that I didn't know what to do. My experience had taught me that you can't just *tell* somebody to stop being depressed. I knew that depression was caused by people having enormous anger inside them, turning that anger inward on themselves, and blaming themselves for what was wrong. I surmised that Germ's friend was angry at his firm for having fired him, had turned on himself, and was now blaming himself for having gotten fired or for not having seen the warning signs.

I knew from experience that you can't give this explanation to depressed people and expect them to accept it and snap out of it. If you try, they will argue with you. They will go to great lengths to convince you of what they are already convinced, that they are a "loser" and there is nothing to be done about it. You can argue with them, pointing out all the good things they have accomplished with their lives, but they will find fault with every good thing they ever did and argue back. They are usually intractable on how rotten and worthless they are.

I racked my brain for how I might be able to help. What *does* work with a depressed person? I reviewed my wife's depression, my depression, but couldn't come up with anything.

I should have remembered that anger expressed is a viable solution. At least it was in my case. But that wasn't the trigger. The trigger was when I remembered something I had accomplished that I couldn't twist into something ugly, no matter how hard I tried. I didn't know Germ's friend at all, so what could I have come up with? The one thing I was certain of was that the anger to be expressed did not have to be the causal anger held inside, tormenting the person. Any anger expressed outwardly, I had found in managing my direct commission salesmen, had an immediate effect of restoring self-confidence. Then they seemed to be equipped to deal with the original problem.

So, the best two solutions I knew of—to make the person angry enough to fight back, or ask a series of easily answered Socratic questions—escaped me. At this moment in time, eleven-thirty that night, I didn't remember any of this.

Germ and I drove over to his friend's home. It was dark. I asked Germ if his friend knew we were coming, and Germ said, "No." I said a silent prayer to God as we got out of Germ's car. "Please, Father, help us help Germ's friend find his way back." Then I added, "Thank You!"

We rang the doorbell and waited. Eventually, the door moved open, slowly. There in the dark was a man in his late forties. He was disheveled, his hair uncombed, face unshaven, and it appeared he had not been bathing. He was in a bathrobe, looking depressed. He stared at us. Germ broke the ice with, "Hi, Maury. How're ya' doin'? This is my friend, Bill. May we come in?"

Maury stepped back, widening the door. He led us through the darkened house to a sunken den. We took chairs, but Maury sat down on the steps that led down into the room. We looked at one another without speaking.

"Well, Maury," Germ started, "my friend, Bill, here has been where you are. He was fired from his job, too. And he lost his wife. She died. He went through some tough times, just as you are, and I wanted you to meet him since you both have so much in common."

No response from Maury. He just stared straight ahead, not focusing on either one of us. That's a usual sign that one is immersed in self-pity and has given up.

"Bill, tell Maury about what you went through and how God helped you out of it," Germ said.

I was at a loss. I was as scared as Germ that this was probably one of Maury's final moments. The responsibility of it was overwhelming and my brain locked up. The enormity of the situation was defeating me. I stammered, starting to tell Maury about my wife and her ordeal, but from there, my memory fails me. Looking back on it now, I remember being anxious, blurting out anything and everything I could think of, not knowing if I was saying the right things or not. I spoke of my experience discovering God. I rambled. I paused once in a while to get a reaction from Maury, but I could not. He sat there, as if frozen.

When I ran out of things to say, Germ picked up and rambled. When he couldn't think of anything more to say, I started over again and rambled. I sensed that we were doing, saying nothing right. But we didn't know what else to do. My Socratic training had failed me. I should have been asking him perception-raising questions, or I should have been challenging him to make him angry, to get the lie inside him out. I could think of none of that. I was panicky.

We talked for hours while Maury sat there staring ahead. Eventually, there was nothing more that could be said, so we thanked Maury for having us over. He stood up, turned, and walked back to the front door with us in tow. He opened the door, we walked out, and he shut it.

Subsequently Germ moved away, so we rarely talked. When we did, the subject of Maury never came up. I guess I was afraid to ask. Years passed. One evening I attended a surprise birthday party Germ's wife threw for him at a local hotel. Since most of Germ's old friends lived down here, she had rented a party room at the hotel, and had sent out invitations, unbeknownst to Germ, as it was to be a surprise.

When Germ and his wife walked in, she threw on the lights and everyone shouted "Surprise!" Germ was taken aback. Laughter broke out and people started to mix. At one point in the evening, we all formed a circle around Germ, who sat in a chair in the middle of the room and opened up the gag gifts. Since he was 50 years old that year, I gave him a giant toothless comb.

While we were standing around, laughing, I became uncomfortably aware that the man next to me was staring at me. His gaze was constant. Finally unable to contend with this another moment, I turned to him and said brusquely, "Can I help you?"

"Don't you remember me, Bill?" he said. I looked him over. Nice suit, well-groomed, gentlemanly in demeanor, a touch of gray at the temples. No, I didn't recognize him.

"Gee, I'm sorry. No, I don't."

"I'm Maury. You visited me one night several years ago at my home with Germ. I was pretty depressed that night. Remember now?"

"Oh, yes, Maury!" I exclaimed, warming up to him now. "How are you doing?"

"You probably don't know it, but you and Germ saved my life that night. I had determined that was going to be the night when I ended it all. But that night, I 'woke up' and realized that I had to fight back."

"Hey, that wasn't me or Germ, pard'ner. *That* was the Big Guy working in your life." I replied.

"Don't I know that!" he said. "I can't even remember one word you or Germ spoke that night. What did get through to me was the kindness. I saw that as pity and it awakened a self-disgust in me. I had finally hit rock-bottom. I asked myself, 'What the hell am I doing to myself here?' No matter how bad I felt about myself, I knew that I was better than this. I got angry with myself and decided that was just enough! I didn't know if I could be successful, but at least I stopped asking myself that question. I determined that anything I tried, even if it resulted in failure, was better than not trying at all. After you guys left that night, I got my act together. I took a shower the next morning, shaved, and dressed. I went out to find a job. I found one, and a new wife. So thank you for that."

"No," I said, "Thank *you*. You just made *my* day. I was happy to be there for you as others have been there for me. But, truthfully, it wasn't me or Germ. It was you, and an insight from God."

"That's right. You and Germ were just the instruments God used that night."

11

The Properties of Miracles

Paralysis Strikes

When my daughter Pamela was seven, she spied her grandfather's violin on our bookshelf and asked to hold it. I explained that it was not a toy, but that I would show her how it worked. I drew the bow across the strings, making a sound like killing a cat. She scowled and protested that couldn't possibly be the way it was supposed to sound. Agreeing, I handed it to her, and said, "Okay, let's see what you can do."

The sweetest sounds emanated from the relic. She asked if she could take it to her room and I agreed. She returned five minutes later and played a song she had heard on the radio. She played it from memory and it was flawless. I just stood in utter amazement. Obviously, this child had a gift from God. From that moment on, the violin consumed her. Playing it professionally would be her career goal.

Her grandfather had had aspirations of being a concert violinist when he was in high school, but World War II came along, and his Old World father, fearing for his son's life, ordered that he not enlist. When he ran off to the Army anyway to be a sergeant, his father confiscated the violin and declared that he was never to play it again without permission, which was never given.

Of course my stepfather was obedient and hoped that his father would relent, but when Grandfather died without retracting his word, that sealed my stepfather's fate with the violin. No amount of explaining by us that Grandfather would have released him from his bond on his deathbed had Stepfather been there was persuasive. Subsequently, he wanted me to study the instrument, but I have trouble playing any musical instrument, including the radio.

Pamela won first chair in every orchestra from grade school through high school every year. When she got to college, she placed seventh chair, first strings. Somewhat of a letdown for her, but not bad for a college freshman competing with juniors and seniors for placement.

Then the unthinkable happened. One night she couldn't hold her food down, so I rushed her to the emergency room, not knowing what was wrong. They diagnosed flu and gave her penicillin. When we got home, she started to feel a numbness come over her legs. She couldn't swallow, and her speech was slurred. She began to cry. When she attempted to walk to her bedroom, her legs gave out. She was scared, so we went back to the emergency room. They thought her symptoms were due to an allergic reaction to the penicillin and gave her a different medicine and we went home again.

The next morning, as I was getting dressed, I heard her scream from her bedroom. I rushed in. She just lay there in bed.

She said, patting her face, "Dad, my face is numb. I have no feeling in it."

"Well, get up and get dressed," I urged, and rushed back to my bedroom, to finish getting dressed. I had no sooner slipped on my shirt, when she screamed again.

"Just about my entire body is numb!" she said.

"Hold on, until I get my shoes on," I said, and rushed back to my bedroom.

Just as I finished, she screamed again. "I'm totally paralyzed, can't even wiggle my toes," she said in a panic. It all happened so fast. I carried her to the car and we sped back to the emergency room.

They tested her and tested her, and finally, hours later said, "We cannot discover what is wrong with her. We need to call in a neurological specialist."

I said, "Do it! Hang the expense. Get the very best neurologist in America, but, please, help my little girl."

"Well, the expense for the best will be pretty high," they said. "Can you afford it?"

"Expense be damned," I declared. "I'll sell my house if I have to."

A few days and much testing later, the neurologist told me, "Your daughter has Guillain-Barré syndrome, a condition that can follow a virus if the immune system is not very strong. Usually 'mono' just slows them down for a short period, but Guillain-Barré is something quite different."

"I don't care what it takes, or what it costs, doctor," I said, "Just, please, help my little girl."

"I'm sorry," he said, "but there is nothing medical science can do. There is no treatment nor medicine that can help her."

"What?" I exclaimed, "You mean she will be paralyzed forever?"

"Oh, no, not necessarily," he explained. "Usually, the symptoms start to reverse themselves and the cure takes place automatically, just like the paralysis came."

"How long does that take, doctor?"

"Well, it depends upon how severe the case is, and I'm sorry to say that your daughter has a very severe case, so I'd estimate that she'll be with us in the hospital for about the next six years."

"Six years! I can't afford a daily hospital bed for six years. I don't even have health insurance. Why, at your daily room rates alone, my house will be gone the first year. Then what? Can't I take care of her needs at home?"

"Oh, no, I'm afraid not. You see, the paralysis is only affecting her outer body at present, but should it seep inside and freeze her heart or lungs, she'd be dead in minutes. Here in the hospital, we could instantly put her on a heart-lung machine and work those organs for her, if it gets to that point, until she starts the recovery process, keeping her alive."

I was stunned. Any hope for my daughter seemed, well, gone. Two thoughts shot through my mind. The first was to wonder if there was any social security or government financial help for her as I was broke. The second was to fall back on my faith and my understanding of how to get miracles from God.

"What is the fastest anybody has ever turned around with Guillain-Barré, Doc?"

"Well, first you have to understand that this is a very rare disease, so we don't have a lot of experience with it. But I did read that there was a preteen boy in Europe at the turn of the century who had a very mild case and he reversed in thirty days."

"Once they reverse and return to normal, they have full dexterity of their limbs, right?"

"Oh, no," the doctor said, "They usually only return to about 80 percent of normal dexterity."

"Oh, doctor, that's just impossible," I exclaimed. "You don't understand. My daughter is a violinist. The violin is the focus of her life. It would break her heart if she couldn't play the violin. And even at 100 percent dexterity, she's got an uphill battle, competing with all of the other violinists out there trying to make a living from their instrument."

"I'm sorry to have to be the one to tell you this, but your daughter will never play the violin again."

That tore it. I couldn't allow that to be. I had no choice but to turn to my faith. Now I do not ascribe to any faith-healing religion. But God would have to kick in once again, for my daughter's sake!

True, I didn't *always* have my miracle requests fulfilled, but I had never failed to get one when I was desperate and my back was up against the wall and there was nowhere else to turn.

I turned to the doctor, looked him square in the eye, and said, "My daughter is walking out of here in 30 days, 100 percent cured, and she *will* play the violin again."

"You're not going to tell her that, are you?" he said.

"Of course, I am. Why wouldn't I?"

"Well, that's just *terrible*," he said, visibly upset. "You'd be the meanest parent in the world if you misled her like that. Why, in 30 days, when she still has shown no improvement, she'll be heartbroken, and could lose the will to live. You'd be responsible for that."

"You have *no* idea what you are dealing with. If you can't get aboard my miracle train, then step aside. I will not have you interfering. First of all, I don't need to tell my daughter *anything* about God's miracles. She has a deeper, more abiding faith, than I do. She already knows it's a done deal. Hear me, and hear me good, doctor: my daughter will walk out of here in 30 days and she will be 100 percent back to normal and she will play the violin again."

Every day after that, I would call the doctor at his office just before his noon lunch break for a progress report. Every day he would say, "No change." This went on for weeks. The only difference I could detect was, that with each passing day, his voice grew quieter, almost as if he had hoped I was right even as he was losing hope with each passing day. In fact, a couple of times he would say things like, "Mr. Tucker, I'm afraid that this case is even worse than I thought. I think you'd better prepare yourself for the worst."

When he would say that, I would get very upset with him, and remind him, "Doctor, where is your faith? I'm telling you again, get off my miracle. If you can't think positively. If you can't believe in advance that a miracle is coming by the end of the month, then get out of the way. I will not have you infecting our faith here with defeatism. My daughter will walk out of your hospital 12 days from now, and she will be 100 percent normal, and she will play the violin, professionally, again."

On the 25th day after Pamela had contracted the disease, her doctor called me. He was excited and the words came out in a rush, "You won't believe it. It's a miracle!"

"Of course I will, doctor, and of course it is."

"No, no, listen. Your daughter—" the doctor was gulping for air. "It's . . . it's a miracle! She's reversing by leaps and bounds."

"Of course she is," I replied calmly. I wasn't excited. After all, what for? This was not news to me. I *knew* this would happen to the core of my being. And that was the secret. I knew in advance that God would not let us down. I knew this miracle had already happened and we were just experiencing it on the date we expected.

Five days later, a mystified neurologist called me and said, "We're releasing your daughter from the hospital today. Technically, I think she's 100 percent recovered, but she'll need some therapy because she still has some numbness that we can work out."

"Thank you, doctor," I replied. "I hope you learned something from this. Never question the power of absolute faith."

There was silence on the other end of the phone. Then he said, "Honestly, I don't know what to make of this . . . never seen anything quite like it . . . I have no explanation. . . ." He trailed off.

"Doctor," I said, "You have eyes, but you do not see. You have ears, but you do not hear."

Pamela went to physical therapy after that. When she auditioned for orchestra re-placement, she earned first chair, first strings. Today she is a professional violinist.

Cancer Strikes

If I know the procedure for getting a miracle, why do I not get all of my miracle requests fulfilled? Simply because I am as human as the next guy, fraught with fear and self-doubt; I lose myself to worry and anxiety even though I know this is the great undoing. I have not given examples of these "failures" because I'm trying to teach you how to *get* miracles, not how to do it wrong. However, when I have needed a great big miracle and there was nothing I could do about the circumstance, I *had* to go to God and put it all in God's hands.

One such occasion was a day in February 1990 when I got a phone call from my mother at St. Mary's Hospital. "You have to get over here to the hospital right away," she pleaded.

"What's the problem?"

"Your father was feeling poorly, so I brought him into the emergency room, and they refuse to talk to me without you here."

I jumped in my car and sped over to St. Mary's. They sent me down to the oncology department. At the time, I didn't know that oncology was the cancer ward. My mother took me to the doctor and I asked him why he wouldn't talk to her.

"Because I have very bad news and I wanted a family member here for her support when I break the news about your father."

"Okay," I said, "What's the problem?"

"Put your arms around your mother's shoulders and hold her tight." I did so. "Your father is dying of cancer and we can do nothing for him." At that, my mother screamed and started to faint, but I held her up.

"Isn't there *something* you can do, doctor?" my mother pleaded.

"I'm sorry, but he's been smoking for over 50 years, and 80 percent of both his lungs are gone. We can't radiate because the amount of radiation and the area we'd have to cover would kill off all his other vital organs. We can't give chemotherapy because, again, the amount of chemo needed would most likely kill him. All we'd accomplish would be to make him sick and miserable for his final days. And we can't operate, because we'd have to remove both lungs and he'd have nothing left to breathe with."

"How much longer does he have, Doctor?" My mother was anxious now, looking for any ray of hope.

"He won't see six months," the doctor said hesitatingly, and nodded to me to hold her once again. I understood that more bad news was coming.

"Doctor," my mother pleaded again, "we have been planning a vacation to Florida for July. Will he be able to go?"

"I don't think you understand," he said. "Your husband will not *see* July."

My mother turned to me, confused by what she was hearing. "What is he saying, Bill?"

"The doctor is trying to tell you, as gently as possible, Mom, that Dad is going to die a whole lot sooner than six months." At this, she screamed again and fainted in my arms. Smelling salts brought her around.

Shaking, she asked, "How much longer does he have, Doctor?" I nodded to him that it was okay to tell her.

"Well, it's impossible to predict, of course, but I don't think he will still be with us three weeks from now. But we can give him something for the pain. We'll probably give him some radiation, but it won't be enough to make a difference."

My mother turned to me and said, "I know that you have a special relationship with God, son. You must save your father."

"Hey, Mom," I said. "I'm not Jesus Christ. What can I do?"

"I know how you brought your daughter back from total paralysis in miraculous time," she said. "And I know about the millions of dollars you've gotten through prayer. Now you *must* cure your father."

So, I turned to the doctor and said, "Okay. My father is all cured now. He won't die. His cancer is gone."

The doctor looked at me as if I was crazy.

"Denial isn't going to help matters here," he replied. "Your father is not going to last out the month."

"Doctor, you have no idea what you are dealing with here, but I'm telling you, my father is cured of his cancer." And with that, my mother and I left the hospital and I put the matter out of my mind. Since it was a done deal, I had no reason to think about it, ask again, or worry whether it would come true or not. I knew the miracle had already taken place, whether any of us could see the physical evidence of it or not.

They gave my father radiation, though surprisingly little. A little dose every six weeks for a while. He lingered on. It might be more descriptive to say that he "limped along." In July, with Dad still sick, my parents went on their Florida vacation.

In October, I was recalled to Navy active duty, since I was a commander in the Naval Reserve, for Operation: Desert Shield, the precursor to Desert Storm. The Navy sent me to Chicago, to "back-fill" for another commander who was sent to Saudi Arabia.

At the end of February 1991, just after the five-day ground war in Iraq ended, I got a phone call at my Navy office. It was my father's oncologist.

"Commander Tucker . . . from Milwaukee?" he asked hesitatingly.

"Yes, this is Bill Tucker."

"Thank God. I've been calling all over the Navy, trying to track you down. You're not going to believe this but—"

"Of course I will, Doctor," I replied before he could finish.

"No, no, listen. You're not going to believe this, but, your father—his cancer is all gone. He's cured. It's a miracle!" he rushed the words out.

"Of course it is, Doctor," I replied, "Where have you been? It happened a year ago, last February, there at the hospital."

"What?" he asked, "I don't follow."

"Doctor, what you have just experienced *is* a miracle. Don't you remember when I told you that my father was cured?"

"Oh, yeah, but I mean *this* is the miracle. I don't know what else to call it." He was clearly not catching on.

My father went to work regularly for the next seven years. Then one day he fell ill again. We took him to a different hospital because his doctor directed us there. When we walked in, his doctor greeted us and then, standing next to my father, his arm over his shoulders, announced to the staff, "Hey, everybody! Here he is. The Miracle Man." The staff, apparently aware of the stories told around the hospital about my father's miraculous cure, broke out in applause.

After completing his physical check of my father, the doctor called me in to consult. "Well, I'm afraid he's had it this time," he said dejectedly. "This time he's got oat-cell cancer, or what's commonly called small cell cancer, and that's the worst kind. It grows *very* rapidly and is the most resistant to treatment."

"Not to worry, Doctor," I said, "He's already cured of it."

The doctor stared at me silently, his eyebrows knitting together in a scowl. Then, hesitatingly, "I . . . don't . . . think . . . so . . . this . . . time."

I laughed out loud. "You didn't think so last time, either, Doc. What do you think about God has changed?"

"Hey," he exclaimed, "I'm not one to knock religion. Whatever works is my motto. But lots of people have faith, and God doesn't cure all of them of cancer."

"Maybe they're not asking God to, Doctor. Did you ever think of that? Maybe they're just fatalists and don't bother God with such a request because they believe in fate. Or maybe they ask, but in their heart, they doubt that God will come through. That would certainly undo it. But look into my eyes, doctor. Do you see any doubt in me?"

"Well, we'll just have to wait and see . . ." he trailed off.

"That doesn't sound like a statement of conviction to me, Doctor. You see, one has to know, absolutely *know in advance* that the miracle has *already* happened, or it can't happen."

The following week the doctor told us that the oat-cell cancer had disappeared. He watched in awe as we walked out of the hospital.

A week later, though, Dad was back in the hospital. The oat-cell cancer had returned. Once again I made my prayer, and the following week dad was declared clear of cancer again. Then a few weeks later it came back, yet again. We were becoming regulars at the hospital.

With each returning bout, the cancer seemed to take more out of my father. His legs swelled up, so he could hardly get around. His breathing was labored. He was miserable. Over the following seven months, the cancer kept disappearing and then returning. I began to feel guilty, as if I was interfering with some greater scheme. I asked God, "How long shall he live? Shall I keep this request up forever? I surely don't want him suffering like this." Then it came to me. It wasn't my call. It wasn't my life. It wasn't my responsibility. It was Dad's . . . and God's. So I said to God, "Please keep him with us as long as possible, but when it is Your time and his time, please, take him gently."

My father had asked the doctor, during his next visit, if he could help him stay alive for a few more weeks. "It's our 50th wedding anniversary, and I'd sure like to celebrate it with my loving wife."

The doctor looked to me. I nodded that it was okay to humor him. The doctor said, "I'll do my best." Then he smiled at my father. Three weeks later we celebrated my parents' wedding anniversary.

My father was now housebound and bedridden, and his swollen legs hurt him very much. One day, soon after their anniversary, while trying to get up to go to the bathroom, he fell and broke his glasses. I helped him back to bed. He looked at me with sorrowful eyes and, crying, said, "Please, son, let me go. It's my time. I don't want to live in pain anymore. Let me die."

I looked heavenward and thought, "We love this man so, but we don't want to keep him beyond his will to live. God, Thy will be done."

We took him back to the hospital. He passed away a few hours later.

When Is It Someone's Time to Go Home to Heaven?

Shortly after my father was cured of his cancer the first time, a friend called me and asked me to come to a bedside vigil for his dying mother. Dozens of friends and family members huddled in the corridor outside her room, as the doctor attended to her inside. I met a bevy of long, sad faces. It appeared as if they were taking the word of the professional—the doctor—that all was lost. My friend drew me aside. "I know of your experience with miracles. Would you be so kind as to pray for my mother?"

"I would be honored to do so. And, please, if we all pray for the same miracle, it happens just that much faster," I answered.

We bowed our heads reverently and prayed. We held vigil for hours out in that corridor. The doctor had said she wouldn't last through the night. Everyone looked worried.

At about two A.M., my friend and I decided to call it a night. We walked out into the street and stopped at the curb. We shook hands to part. He thanked me for having come. I smiled. "Anytime. Only too glad to be here with you."

As he walked to his car, he turned and said, "Oh well, she had a nice life." I could feel my heart break, and the hot tears welled up in my eyes. I knew at that moment that she was gone. The next morning we found out that she had died at that exact moment.

I guess she was supposed to. At least, that's what everyone seemed to *believe*.

What Is a Miracle?

What is a miracle and what does it mean to ask correctly for one? I define a miracle as a great big freebie, something beyond the realm of the known, an event that defies logic or goes against what scientists call the world of natural order.

Let me give you an example. My son, then age 13, and I were walking out of a store and I was enlightening him on God and miracles. As always happens whenever I do this, God steps in and gives a practical demonstration. Matt was getting in the car, a four-door sedan, the kind that has metal framing around the window. He had his left hand on the top of the door, and pulled the door shut with his right hand, slamming the door closed with his left hand caught between the car frame and door frame. We both heard the door latch click, shut solid. Matt screamed, and I immediately reached across him to open the door. I expected to see a mangled, bloodied stump for a hand. But, miraculously, Matt's hand didn't have a scratch.

We sat there in the car, amazed. Then I tried to close the door on my own hand to see if there was any give at all. The closest I could come was to within one inch of closing. There was no space between the door and window frames. I then stuck a piece of paper between the door and car frame, and closed the door. I tried to pull the paper out. It wouldn't budge. How could Matt's hand have escaped unscathed? It had to be a miracle.

We tend to think in terms of absolutes and cause and effect. We think that certain things must happen in a logical, progressive order for other events to follow. But miracles are outside that earthly understanding. If we get a miracle—some wonderful unexplainable thing happens—we know Who is responsible, and we thank God. Some of us burn candles of thankfulness. Some rush to church to show appropriate appreciation. Some who profess not to believe in God or miracles just smile and shrug their shoulders, and attribute it to good luck. That's okay. All of them are "okay." Whether we choose to acknowledge God or miracles, I think, doesn't really matter to God. God is there, whether we choose to believe in God or not, and God will go on about God's task of providing for us, quietly and lovingly.

I believe, because I have experienced it, that it is possible for us to turn away from a potential miracle by not believing that God hears us or not believing that God is sympathetic or not believing God is proactive in our lives.

As has been noted, in Mark 11:24, John 2:1–11, and other places throughout the Old and New Testaments, the message of God's love is repeated over and over again. Jesus said, "Therefore I tell you, whatever you ask in prayer, believe that you have received it, and it will be yours." But He doesn't stop there. He puts a couple of caveats on that lesson that are also part of making a miracle happen, and they mustn't be overlooked. "And whenever you stand praying, forgive, if you have anything against anyone; so that your Father also who is in heaven may forgive you your trespasses."

I think that if we skip any of the three parts of God's promise to perform miracles in our lives, we will be disappointed and think that God either doesn't hear us or doesn't care to answer our prayers. But if we do what God asks of us, can God possibly *not* deliver our miracles? If God doesn't deliver our miracle request, then either God is a liar or God doesn't exist. Since neither is true, then God *must* deliver our miracle to us, mustn't God? After all, God promised. As God says in the *Conversations with God* books, and as Jesus said on the Mount, "Or what man of you, if his son asks him for a loaf, will give him a stone? . . . If you then . . . know how to give good gifts to your children, how much more will your Father who is in heaven give good things to those who ask him?"

Since God is all-loving, God would not, could not, refuse us if we truly *believe,* if we take the position that we *know* it has happened already.

Of the three steps to a miracle, the hardest one for believing human beings seems to be the second, believing in advance. Friends have told me, "Oh, I *do* believe." So, I ask them, "Okay, if you think you do, faith-fully and fully, believe, then let's ask God to have someone walk into this restaurant in the next five minutes and lay a bag with one million dollars on the table and tell us it's ours, no strings attached. Shall we do this?"

I usually get a blank stare. No one, it seems, wants to test God to this degree. After all, if it doesn't happen, there may be no God. Then fear would conquer all. I am not making light of their faith. I have been where they are and I have done this. I asked God to give me a million dollars, free and clear, in a 14-day period. On the 14th day after making my request, a bank gave me one million dollars. When they handed me the check, the bank president said, "Now, don't worry if you lose our million dollars. We won't hold it against you. We do this all the time. Most of these good ideas fail. But when one hits, we're more than com-pensated for the ones that don't."

Since I am the one who said to God "in 14 days," how else could that event be explained? Chance? Luck? Coincidence? You can believe what you like, but I know what I believe. When you can invoke such luck on demand, I will be happy to hear how you did it.

When we come to that moment of truth, when we must confront our belief in advance of hoping for a miracle and it doesn't happen, who is to blame? Who is infallible? Which, us or God, never doubts? As the old cartoon strip character Pogo used to say, "We have met the enemy, and he is us."

So if we are living in fear and causing our own undoing, how can we find perfect faith in advance? I have three suggestions as to how all of us can get our miracles. First, I have always been able to trust in God when I had nowhere else to turn and desperately needed a miracle. Second, I found that if after asking for something I absolutely need I say "Thank You," I feel a weight lift from my shoulders as I pass my caring onto God. After all, who would say "Thank you" unless the deed was already done? Then I put it out of my head. I forget about it, lest I fall into the trap of worrying.

Third, I have a new understanding of what a miracle is after reading Neale Donald Walsch's *Conversations with God* books. Think about this for a moment: *Everything* is a miracle. Every act, every action, every event in our lives is just as we *believe* it will be. If we believe our loved one will be cured of cancer, they will be. If we believe that they won't be cured of cancer, they won't be. It is our belief that causes all to happen. God answers all beliefs, even the ones we don't think we are "asking" for.

You've probably heard the admonition, "Be caresul what you pray for—you just might get it." I would suggest that we modify this to, "We get what we believe, so be careful what you believe, for as you believe, so shall you receive."

Creating the "Wrong" Miracle

Here are a couple of examples to illustrate these points. During one of my many financial crises, I realized I had the power to call upon God to solve my financial worries with a lottery ticket. Our state did not have a lottery in those days, so I drove to Illinois to buy the winning lottery ticket. After all, I only needed one, and I reasoned that if I asked God, He would direct me to the winning ticket.

I stopped at the first lottery outlet I found. I bought one ticket—obviously the winning ticket—and started the long drive back home. I was beaming. My financial worries were now over for all time.

But, as I drove along, guilt started to overcome me. I began to worry. I worried that I was defaming the miracle process that I had been entrusted with. I worried that I was using God for my own personal gain. It didn't occur to me that maybe God *wanted* me to have the winning ticket.

I worried for the entire trip home. I thought about all the starving children in the world. I worried that they were more deserving and needful of such a windfall. I worried that maybe I was taking food from their mouths. I thought about all the sick people in the world to whom the miracle of a winning ticket could make all the difference. Those thoughts brought me to reflect on my life and how blessed I had been. The guilt was crushing now.

By the time I got home, I had come to disdain the winning ticket in my pocket. I felt ashamed that I had ever undertaken the trip in the first place. As I stepped out of the car, I looked heavenward and said out loud, "Father, if there is someone else you want to have this winning ticket, please give it to them."

I should have known that there was no reason to check the lottery numbers in the paper the next day. I should also have known not to be surprised or disappointed that none of the numbers on my ticket were printed in the newspaper. I looked. I was surprised. And I was disappointed. It wasn't until weeks later, when I reflected on my bad luck, that I realized I got exactly what I asked for. I got what I expected. I can only surmise that the winning ticket did go to someone who needed it more than I because that was my prayer, after all, wasn't it?

Logic Gives It Away

Why did I give the winning lottery ticket away? That I had the winning ticket in my possession I do not doubt. I willingly gave it up. But why? Love for my fellow man? Sure. Empathy for those in (greater) need? Of course. For those who do not know how to get a miracle and need one desperately? Possibly. Because that's what God wanted me to do? Sounds like a good reason to me. Because I wanted to? Apparently.

But what if it is bigger than that? Did I doubt my worthiness? Don't we all, at times? The Catholic Church used to sell absolutions as a ticket into heaven that a rich man could buy. But Martin Luther raised the Church's perception that *all* get into heaven *only* by the Grace of God. And God does not withhold grace from anybody, regardless of the life they live while on Earth. Why? Because God loves *all* of God's Creations. How could God not? There is no wiggle room to exclude anyone in "all-loving" that I can see.

I believe that God and I and you are all working together. If I wanted the winning lottery ticket to go to someone less fortunate than myself, then it stands to reason that God wanted that, too. Which came first? My desire or God's? Did God plant that thought in my head? Does it matter? Whatever we believe, all I know is that *believing* makes it so.

12

Believing in Miracles Makes Them So

The "Appearance" of Bad News

Sometimes, what we perceive to be very bad news enters our life. A seemingly terrible event befalls us. At those moments, we may find ourselves railing against God. It has been my experience that if we wait long enough to see God's plan unfold, we discover that the "bad" thing had to happen for the "good" things to follow, or they might not have followed at all.

In fact, there is—and we can see it if we look—a seemingly causal relationship between what we thought was the bad thing and the eventual good thing coming to pass. I'm sure if you reflect on something in your past that you gnashed your teeth about, and maybe cursed a seemingly unfeeling Almighty over, you will see that the good events that followed were almost certainly causally related to that event that so troubled you at the time.

What is good to remember when something that appears to be devastatingly bad happens is that we should view it as a blessing. It's okay. Whatever Thy will is, Lord, is okay with me. That's a prayer that can give you much peace of mind at those low moments.

Usually, such good-bad linked events are separated by a significant period of time, such as months or even years. I had one happen pretty quickly. In fact, had it not been for my understanding of God and

God's miracles, I probably would have been gnashing my teeth instead of laughing.

Asking to Be Fired

At the time of this example, I was managing a large, two-level enclosed mall. I thought it to be a "velvet prison"—nice income, good job, lots of authority, the responsibility I thrive on, but limiting and stifling. I was very good at my job, and liked it, for that matter. I had 150 employees, and I enjoy managing. But I felt unfulfilled. I wanted to do something greater. The entrepreneurial spirit hadn't been dampened in me with my magazine experience; it was whetted.

I designed a computer program that would help a Realtor sell homes in one day based on The Socratic Method. That's a departure from the average 60 days it usually takes a Realtor to get a buyer to make an offer. Realtors find themselves making recommendations on which home to buy. This leads them to frequently talk up a particular house without much knowledge as to whether it is the right house or the best house for the buyers. They have it backwards. Realtors perceive that their job is to sell homes. It's not, and the introduction of the Multiple Listing Service proved that 30 years ago. Their job is to sell buyers. In order to do that, they must know as much as possible about what the buyer wants, needs, and can afford.

But they don't bother to ask because, even if they did have this information, they couldn't do anything with it. The Multiple Listing Service computer program is not designed to search for dozens of home features and analyze that data. A program that could is what I designed.

Since I am not a computer programmer, I needed to find one to help make my dream a reality. I called IBM Business Solutions, but they wanted more money than I could have saved in a lifetime, and, basically, I did not have any discretionary money to invest anyway. In fact, I was living from paycheck to paycheck. As I sat at my desk one day, I looked up at the ceiling, and I said, "Tell you what, Big Guy, You get me a computer programmer for free, and I'll have the nerve to quit this job, and just *expect* that You'll see that my software business can support me."

At that moment, the door of my office opened, and my boss, the vice president, walked in. "I'm sorry to have to tell you this, Bill, but you're fired."

"What!" I was shocked. "Haven't I been doing a good job?"

"Oh, absolutely. You've done remarkable work. It'll be hard to get along without you, although you *have* solved virtually all of the problems I was hoping you would when I hired you. But things are running smoothly now. It's just that my best friend, who lives in Texas, has called me, and his business has gone bankrupt. He needs a job, so I gave him yours."

I burst out laughing. He was as perplexed as I would have been if I didn't understand how God works. When he left my office, I looked heavenward and said, "No, no! You're supposed to get me a programmer *before* I lose my job." I laughed because I knew God would not let me down.

My termination notification period passed without incident except that I did even more good work for the company. I didn't bother looking for a new job. After all, God "owed" me a programmer. God "owed" me one because I was believing that God would give me one as a miracle.

The day I was packing up my belongings to clear out my office, there came a knock. It was an old friend. He was an insurance agent whom I had not seen for ten years. "Ron!" I exclaimed. "What are you doing here? Are you in town on business?"

"Yes, I was," he said, "and I just finished up. I had some time on my hands, so I thought I'd stop by and renew old acquaintances. I wanted to see your new office."

"Well, take a quick look around. I'm on my way out the door right now," I laughed. "By the way, what're you doing these days, buddy?"

"Well, I'm really excited," he exclaimed. "You know how I've been in the insurance business for the past 25 years? Well, I've joined a new company owned by an old friend. I've been selling computer software programs for the past six months, and am loving it."

"What a coincidence," I said. "I'm just about to launch a software company. I need a programmer. I just need to find one who will work for free." I laughed.

"*Not* a problem," he declared. "My boss will write your program for you, I'm sure, for a piece of the action."

"Why would he do that for me?" I asked.

"Because he owes his career and his success to your sister. She gave him a job when he was desperate and nobody else would take a chance on him. That start got him to where he is today. I think he'll want to pay that favor back. We can meet with him tomorrow."

Prayer answered, just as I knew *in advance* that it would be. I looked up to my ceiling and mouthed a "Thank You." We met the next day and the deal was sealed.

Our State of Perfection

In truth, as Jesus said, we are all perfect. After all, we are made in God's image, aren't we? So how could we be anything less than perfect? Our problem is that we don't believe that this is so, and we act accordingly. You see, we cannot be *not* perfect. So we become perfectly wrong on purpose.

This truism was driven home to me one day when I was watching a Milwaukee Bucks basketball game. The score was 97 to 98 in favor of the Bucks and there were only seconds left on the clock. The other team scored a basket, putting them ahead 99 to 98. A hoop shot for two points was the only hope the Bucks had. As the ball fell through the basket after the opposing team's shot, it fell into the hands of a Bucks player. He instantly turned and threw the ball the entire length of the court toward the opposite hoop. Swish, the ball fell through the hoop just as the ending buzzer sounded. The arena burst into bedlam at the unbelievable shot that won the game.

Unbelievable? Why wasn't it believable? After all, this was an accomplished athlete who had spent thousands of hours practicing and perfecting his basketball skills. Of course, we rarely see such perfection even from experts in any walk of life. That's when it struck me. This basketball player did not have time in that one second to doubt himself. He just assumed he could make the shot, so he did. His perfectly created eye and his perfectly trained arm coordinated together with absolute faith in his ability to do the task *without doubt or fear* could render no other outcome.

A few days later, I was sitting at my computer and printed out a page with a mistake on it. Frustrated, I crumpled the paper up and tossed at the wastebasket only a foot away and missed. How could I miss? I picked up the wad of paper and threw it again at the wastebasket. It hit the rim and bounced off, again missing. I was now angry with myself. I picked it up a third time and threw it again. I was close enough that I could have just reached over and placed it in the basket, but now it had become a point of pride. I missed again! But this time, I noticed something. I had been looking at the hole, but at the last split second, my eye shifted and looked at the rim and sure enough, I hit exactly what I was aiming for—the rim.

I thought about this. How could I hit that rim three times in a row and miss that big hole every time? After all, isn't the rim so much smaller that if I had been trying to hit the rim, my paper ball would have accidentally fallen into the big hole? And that's when it struck me. I was hitting what I was aiming for—the rim. I was doubting my ability to be perfect. So my eye and arm shifted at the last second to miss the hole, to prove to myself that I am as imperfect as I believed I was.

This time, I concentrated on looking at a tiny spot in the middle of the wastebasket. The area seemed to expand to 100 times its size. Swish. The paper ball sank directly into the middle of the wastebasket without coming near the sides or the rim. To test my theory, I moved the wastebasket five feet away. Swish. Then ten feet away. Swish. Then 15 feet. Swish. Then 20 feet away. Swish. I threw the paper ball ten more times at that distance and I made every shot.

"Aha!" I thought. We are perfect. We just tell ourselves that we aren't, and since we cannot be wrong, we take the action necessary to prove to ourselves that we *can* fail by being perfectly wrong. We can't escape our perfection, just as we can't escape our miracles. God promises to give us all of the miracles we want. So everything in our lives, every action, every act, is a miracle. When we get cancer, that's a miracle because we consciously or subconsciously ask for it. How? By being fearful that we might get it. By being fearful, we draw the experience to ourselves.

Some people smoke cigarettes for 60 years and never get lung cancer. Others never smoke, but get lung cancer. How does that happen?

Where is the logic in that? When we get a million dollars, we recognize that as a miracle because we consider that unbelievably good news. In short, we get what we believe we will get, what we believe we deserve. If we believe that we are imperfect and do not deserve good things, we get that—what we need to get to prove to ourselves that we aren't perfect and aren't deserving of good things.

This brings to mind another occasion when that point was driven home to me. I had a housekeeper at one time, a girl who constantly doubted herself. That attitude was easy to trace back to her father, who constantly had expressed doubt in her abilities since she was born. She had heard nothing for the first 22 years of her life but that she was incapable. She confided in me that she had never learned to drive, in fact, was incapable of learning to drive. I assured her that driving was easy, and the proof was that virtually everybody learned to drive, regardless of their level of intelligence. I offered to teach her. After much encouragement, she finally agreed to try. That should have been my first clue things were not going to go well. When we say we will *try*, we are assuming a potential for failure. Ergo, we fail.

I drove us out to a lonely stretch of highway and when there were no other cars on the road, I put her behind the wheel. She started out well, accelerating smoothly, driving straight. Then, all of a sudden, she started steering the car toward the ditch. "Turn the wheel!" I shouted. She did. She turned the wheel even more toward the ditch. "No, no! The other way," I shouted, panicky now. She continued to turn the wheel even more the wrong way in the direction of the ditch until we ended up in the ditch. She was mystified as to how this had happened yet she wasn't surprised. She *expected* to wind up in the ditch. She *expected* to fail. She *had* to fail to prove to me and herself that she was short of the perfection of God.

This has brought up the need to understand just how this planet we live on works. In order to illustrate the truth of it, one must start with an understanding that "everything on planet Earth is *backwards* from reality." Not some things. Not most things. *Every* thing. Let me tell you a little story that explains the concept.

13

The Secret of Life

This story is a history lesson about America that hasn't happened yet. How do I know? Because I am from the future. In fact, I am not from Earth, but from another planet. As America was about to prove Einstein's theory about the curvature of space by sending an astronaut into space, my planet was sending me on a similar mission. I have come to earth from the planet of Nevaeh. . . .

The Planet of Nevaeh

Einstein's general theory of relativity says many things. It says that space is curved and that time compresses with speed. So, the theory goes, if man were able to leave Earth on a spaceship that could travel at the speed of light, he would travel the curve of space, and eventually land right back on Earth and be only about 20 years older. Thousands of years would have passed on Earth, and all of his friends would be long gone.

Humans accomplish this feat about 20 years into our future. America invents a rocket that can travel at the speed of light, and it will be decided to send an astronaut off into space to prove Einstein's theories, much the same way Columbus sailed to find a new route to the Far East, or Magellan sailed to prove the world is round.

The astronaut was launched in the year 2020 A.D., but he was only gone for about two weeks when he crash-landed. "Oh, no," he thought. "I couldn't have circumnavigated the entirety of space in only two weeks. I must have bumped into an asteroid or something, and now I'll be stuck here the rest of my life."

So he climbed down out of his rocket. Sure enough, it was crinkled. It couldn't fly anymore. So, he looked around to see where he was going to be marooned for the rest of his life, and, lo and behold, he was back on Earth. And, luck of luck, he had crash-landed just on the outskirts of his hometown. He decided, since dusk was falling, to walk home and spend the night, and then call the air base in the morning to tell them that he must have flown straight up for a week, retrograded, and then flown back to Earth for a week.

As he neared the edge of town, he noticed that the sign that should have said "Welcome to Smallville" was written as "Ellivllams ot Emoclew." The words were right, but everything was backwards. How odd, he thought. As he passed each street sign, he noticed that the names of the streets were correct but spelled backward. "Main" was now "Niam," "Elm" was "Mle," and so on. What is going on here? he asked himself. It must be those college kids up to their pranks, he reasoned.

When he got to the center of town, he noticed that all the cars were driving on the wrong side of the road. People in restaurants were eating with their left hands. Oh, some were using their right hands, but the majority were left-handed. Perplexed, he strolled down "Niam" Street, and spied his old girlfriend across the street. He rushed over to meet her. She didn't know him at all. But, in conversation with her, he discovered that he was *not* back on Earth after all, but instead was on another planet called Nevaeh.

He became depressed. Since he was now marooned on this strange planet that appeared to be Earth, but wasn't, and since his rocket ship was crinkled, he realized that he would be stuck here forever. He decided that he would have to acclimate and start a new life on this planet. He took a job as a salesman and spent his free time learning as much as he could about this strange new world.

It turned out that the planet had the same number of continents as his Earth. They even looked like Earth's continents, but they were on the other side of the planet and were shaped backward from Earth's.

Their "American" continent had Florida on the West Coast, and the California-shaped landmass on its East Coast. How unusual, he thought.

He also discovered that this planet had the same number of "beings"—6 billion—inhabiting it. Then he began to learn some surprising things about this strange place. They didn't have famine. They had the same amount of food as Earth, and the same number of people, but they had a much better distribution system. In fact, on this planet he didn't see any evidence of anger, hate, judgments, or even war. Everybody seemed to get along together pretty well.

The company he worked for had an unusual setup. The company's organizational chart looked like this:

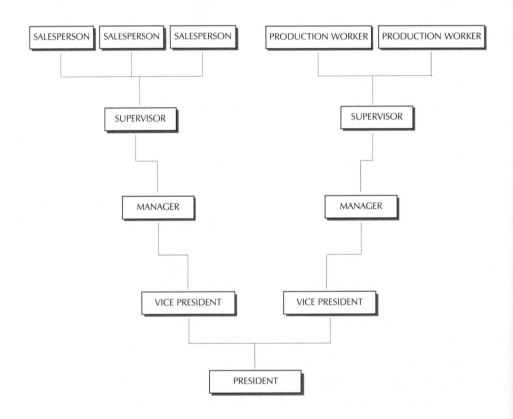

When he asked about it, noting that it was apparently upside down or in seemingly reverse order of importance, his company president explained it by first asking a few questions. "On such a chart, the important people are at the top, and the further down you go, those are the less important people, aren't they?"

Of course, our astronaut agreed, that is how such charts are designed.

"So who are the most important people in this company?" he asked. The astronaut pointed out that, in his experience, the president was the most important person in a company, because he is responsible for everybody else having a job.

The president asked him, "But who brings the operating money into the company?" Salesmen and production workers, said the astronaut. The president next said, "If there are no successful salesmen and production workers, can there even *be* a company?" The astronaut acknowledged that there couldn't be.

"If the salesmen and production workers are the ones keeping the company alive," the president explained, "then they are the most important people in the company, and go at the top. Everyone else in the company—supervisors, managers, vice presidents, and president—all serve to support the salesmen and production workers. Therefore, they are increasingly less important to the organization the further down the chart you go because they have less and less influence on the greatest number of people. They exist only to keep the salesmen and production workers producing income."

"But," protested the astronaut, "the bosses give the orders, and orders come down from the top."

"And where do the questions come from?" the president challenged him.

"Up from the bottom, where I am," the astronaut said.

"Exactly!" the president said. "The salesmen at the top bring in the orders from the customers, and the production workers fill those orders. That's why they're both at the top. Support personnel, like managers, don't 'boss' people around. They ask the questions to get their salesmen and production workers to think critically and solve their own problems. Only when someone's brain is fully working, and they are taking responsibility for their own challenges, will they learn and increase in their skills. So, the job of the support staff is to help the most important people in the company do their job with questions, not orders."

This made some sort of convoluted sense to the astronaut that he couldn't argue with, so he dropped the subject. The president added that was how the salesmen were successful with their customers, the only people higher in importance to the company than the salesmen and production workers. "Our salesmen," he explained, "*ask* our customers their problems and needs, and then fill those needs by taking orders. Our production people *ask* the salesman how they can best serve the salesman's customers, and fulfill those needs with our products.

"The whole system works very well. Can you imagine what a mess it would be if it was the other way around with salesmen trying to tell their customers what they should buy? Or, management trying to tell salesmen how to tell anything to their customer? Why, we'd fail overnight. Sales would not be coming in and production wouldn't give a hang what the salesmen's customers wanted. Support staff as bosses? The support staff would then be out of touch with reality, and would get an inflated idea of their importance to the company, and all would be lost. Why, I can even imagine our support staff calling themselves executives, and taking the biggest salaries and longest lunch hours and swaggering around with fancy cars. Utter nonsense! Nobody would be listening to anybody else. How would things get accomplished that way?"

The astronaut left to ponder these perceptions. The next day, he returned to the president's office with more questions. "I'm not sure I understand your philosophy," he began. "Aren't we supposed to take responsibility for our own work?"

The president's eyes rolled heavenward. "Let me ask you," he said, "in two words, what does a farmer do?"

"Grows food," was the astronaut's answer.

"And, in two words, what does a doctor do?"

"Heals people," came the quick reply.

"And in two words, what does a teacher do?"

"Teaches people," said the astronaut growing in confidence at his ability to summarize these complex responsibilities into only two words.

"And a salesman?" the president asked.

"Sells people!" the astronaut responded.

"I don't know where you're getting your information," the president said, "but I can tell you've got an awful lot to learn. First of all, a farmer does not grow food. A farmer finds God's seeds lying on the ground, and he plants them in God's ground, and then he waits while God's rain and God's sunshine fall upon the seeds and cause them to grow. Then, all the farmer does is cut it down. The farmer can't create anything. He is only a reaper—a taker.

"A doctor can't 'heal' anybody, and they'd be the first to admit that. All the doctor does is set a broken bone, then God knits the bone and heals it. Or the doctor finds some unnatural growth, like cancer, and cuts the malignant growth out. Then he waits while God causes the cells in the flesh to regrow and heal the cut body.

"A teacher can't teach anyone anything if the student is not listening or does not understand because they have not put their brain into gear. A teacher can offer information in the most entertaining way they know, but it is up to the student to understand, to put their brain that God gave them to work in figuring out how math or science or language works.

"And a salesman certainly cannot 'sell' anybody anything that they don't want or need to buy. You have to understand how this planet works if you want to be a salesman here. All you can do is help facilitate the customer in discovering for themselves whether they want or need your product as the perfect solution for their problem, and to understand if they can afford your solution or not. Until you start to trust that God is your sales-Helper, helping people discover their own needs and solutions, because you are doing God's work for your customers, you will not be successful."

The next day, the astronaut was back in the president's office for some personal advice. "Can you explain to me," he asked, "what the Planet of Nevaeh does with its ax murderers? You lock them up in prison for life or kill them, right?"

The president just looked heavenward. He couldn't believe his ears. "How would *that* serve anybody?" he asked. "Let me ask you a few questions," he continued, obviously used to raising his salesmen's perceptions by asking questions and getting them to think for themselves. "What causes a person to become an ax murderer in the first place?"

"I don't know."

"Of course you do," the president protested. "You just haven't asked yourself the question because you assume that you don't know the answer. So, to help you figure it out, answer me this: How does one get love?"

The astronaut thought about this for a while, then answered, "By giving it."

"Okay," the president agreed. "Then, to give something away to another person, you have to have extra of it yourself, don't you?"

"Yes," agreed the astronaut.

"Then who must the one giving away love first?"

"Oneself?" ventured the astronaut.

"Okay, if someone is giving away hate, whom do they have to hate first?"

"Oneself?"

"So, ax murderers, who are giving hate, don't love themselves. Is that what you're telling me?"

"Yes," said the astronaut.

"So, they give hate to others by hitting them over the head with an ax, probably in a fit of rage," he continued.

"Yes."

"Then I guess you knew what causes people to become ax murderers all along. Now, let me ask you, if we think that killing is wrong, how could we justify doing that to another human being, by killing them? Wouldn't that say something about our insecurity, about how we feel about ourselves, inside?"

"I guess. . . ." the astronaut agreed, as he pondered the strange way the conversation was going.

"Tell me," the president continued, "what would be accomplished for the ax murderer by putting him behind bars for the rest of his life? Would he learn to love himself in there? Moreover, would he learn that we love him, as a fellow human being, as deserving of our love?"

"Of course not," the astronaut was now ready to make his case, "but, while I agree that he's not going to be rehabilitated in prison, at least he'd be off the streets where he couldn't kill anybody again."

"Then it would be necessary to keep him locked up for life with no hope for parole, because he surely isn't learning love in prison, nor love for himself, is he? And if freed, he would surely have the same personal problem of not loving himself—isn't that true?"

"I guess so," the astronaut said.

"Okay, I'll now tell you what we do with an ax murderer when we catch him. We put him on a train and send him to a small town somewhere else on the planet. When the train pulls into the station, there is a brass band playing 'For He's a Jolly Good Fellow,' and there are about 150 townspeople there to greet him, and hug him, and tell him they love him. Then they give him a free house, a car, a job, furniture, and a television set. There are no fences around the town and no locks on any doors. He is free to run away again if he wants to because we trust him."

"But what happens if he decides to go next door and take his neighbor's television set?"

"Oh, that's okay," the president answered. "Nobody would be angry, if that's what you're implying. They would just wait until he went to sleep and take their television set back. There are no locks anywhere, you see. No matter how many times he stole their set, they'd always take it back. No harm done. Until he got tired of the game and bought himself a second television set."

"Okay, point well made. But what if he went into the unlocked hardware store in town and took an ax, and then when he stole his neighbor's television set, he whacked them with the ax so they couldn't come and take it back?"

"We would go and get him again."

"But you said there were no fences around the town, so he could commit murder and then run away again."

"And we'd go get him again!" the president declared. "This time, when we caught him, we'd put him on another train to another small town, where a brass band would be playing, and the townspeople would be there to open their hearts to him. . . ."

"Yeah, yeah," the astronaut protested, "I get it. But, you've now got two more dead people—*good* people—and this loser is going to get away with it again!"

"*Good* people?" the president questioned. "Loser?" he asked the astronaut to think it through. "All people are God's creation. All people are

God's children. God loves each and every one of them. How could we do less? But I think you're missing the point. When we sincerely show him that we love him, he begins to understand that we know he is a good person deep down inside; he starts to understand that he is lovable. He learns that someone, somewhere, falsely taught him that he was not. Then he starts to learn to love himself. When that happens, he starts giving love back. It's simple logic. Your logic, if I am to believe you, as to what causes a person to be loved or be an ax murderer in the first place.

"But I understand where you're coming from. You are *afraid*, so you want to remove him from society as someone who can't be rehabilitated, or isn't worthy of being rehabilitated. You aren't dealing with him or his crime at all, are you? You are dealing with your fear of him. 'And which of you by being anxious can add one cubit to his span of life?' as one of our favorite residents said long ago. We *all* die and *we know* that we do not die until our appointed hour. So what is there to fear? More importantly, what is there to be gained, in terms of reducing the number of ax murders, if we learn to really love our fellow men, *all* our fellow men, and teach them to love themselves, and us?"

The astronaut left to ponder these things. "This place is nuts," he decided. "It's exactly backward from the way we think on Earth. Interesting, hmmm . . . this planet is an exact reflection of Earth, a mirror image."

And then it hit him like a thunderbolt! *This* planet isn't the mirror image of Earth. *Earth* is the mirror image. This place does it right. It's *Earth* that's got *everything* backward. Earth is the phony place. *This* is the real world. After that realization, he was happy to be stuck on the Planet of Nevaeh for the rest of his life because, as he realized, "In the beginning, God created *Nevaeh* and Earth. . . ."

If you want to explore this concept, that everything on Earth is backwards, ask yourself questions about your core beliefs. Discover the real answers. The truthful answers. *Your* answers. Begin to see the truth of things on Earth. It will expand your mind. It will lead you down the road of discovery and enlightenment.

Ask yourself, "What in Christ's teachings did the Crusaders see that assured them that Christ wanted them to kill unbelievers in His name?"

Was that correct? In line with Christ's teachings? I cannot, for the life of me, find even one passage, one sentence, one word from Christ other than "love everybody." In fact, He specifically went out of his way to express "love your enemies and turn the other cheek." We have even taken and turned His word backward. Oh, you're not a Crusader, so of course, you wouldn't misinterpret that and turn His teachings backwards? Then, I guess you've never become frustrated and angry with another person on the freeway, at work, or (God forbid) at home? Turning the other cheek is not just for strangers and enemies. That which we do for our enemies shouldn't we do even more for our loved ones?

Here are a couple of questions you can ask yourself to get your philosophical motor running: *If* what I said is true, that everything is backwards, ask yourself . . .

If we call it *Life,* what is it, *really?*

And, if we call it *Death,* what is it, really?

There are so many, many things, concepts, ideas, that we hold near and dear that are just simply backward from the truth, that this is an exercise without end. But the deeper one delves into it, the more light of understanding beams down on our human psychology, and gives us the power over our lives, and helps us to use that power to benefit ourselves and our fellow man.

14

How We Hurt Our Miracles

The Hardest Part Is Doing Nothing

I have found that the hardest part is doing nothing when there is so much that needs to be done. Now that we know what is required of us, as our part of getting miracles, what aren't we allowed to do? We are *not allowed* to do anything in furtherance of getting our miracle. That's sometimes as hard as Believing in Advance.

Let's say you are facing a catastrophe, something over which it would seem logical that you might, or should, have control, but for whatever reason, it has gotten away from you. Say you are facing foreclosure on your home. You lost your job a year ago and have not gotten another. You have a huge debt. Your back is to the wall. There is nothing you can do. So you turn to God and ask God's indulgence in providing you with a miracle, a financial windfall, to save your house.

You pray and ask God to deliver you this miracle. You search your heart for any you have enmity against, and dig deep down within your soul and forgive them their trespasses against you. All that's left is to Believe in Advance that God *will* deliver God's miracle to you, 100 percent, knowing that 99.9 percent of faith is *zero* faith. You either have it or you don't. If you don't, you'd better not kid yourself. You'd better start making arrangements to move, because the miracle isn't going to happen. God *promises* that it *will* happen, as you ask, if you believe in advance, *absolutely*. *Believing in Advance* = KNOWING you already have the miracle.

So, you ask and name a date for the financial windfall to arrive. Here's a list of what you *can't* do in the meantime:

1. You cannot *worry* about whether God will come through or not. That is only proof that you have *not* turned it over to God, but are hanging onto it.

2. You cannot pray and ask again tomorrow. That, too, is a demonstration that apparently you didn't believe the first time you prayed and asked, or else why would you have to ask again? That is your fear of failure coming out, your doubt that God exists and answers all prayers. And, if you do pray for the same miracle twice, what's to reassure you on the third day? Shouldn't you then have to pray and ask again that day, and the next, and the day after that? Which day will be the "real" prayer that you believe will come to pass?

3. You cannot help God out. Yes, I know that it is hard not to want to step in and participate in helping your miracle occur. Maybe you should go to the bank and plead with them; maybe they'll cut you some slack, you reason. Maybe you should go look for that windfall, knocking on doors and asking? . . . Maybe you should call your rich Uncle Charlie, the one who pinches every penny and never helps anybody. Maybe God will soften Uncle Charlie's heart. You cannot do these or myriad other things you might think of to help God out. If God wants Uncle Charlie to help you out, Uncle Charlie will call you without any prompting at your end.

God doesn't *need* our help. God is quite capable of performing God's miracles all alone. Doing any of these proactive things will actually "kill" your miracle. When you interfere with God's work, you deny God the opportunity to perform.

As an analogy, when your hands are on the wheel of a bus careening down a mountain, you are keeping God's hands off the wheel. Admittedly, it's hard to take your hands off the wheel as the bus appears to be out of control, and the precipice is only inches away. It would take an enormous act of faith—some would say foolhardiness—to release the wheel and *trust* that God will take over the steering.

If at that moment, you turn fatalist and say to yourself, "Okay, I'm going to take a chance on God, and if God steers this bus to safety, I'll live, and if God doesn't, I'll die, but at least I will have tried"—then please don't take your hands off the wheel because you will surely die. That reasoning is not a statement of faith. "Trying" is for fools. "Trying" implies a potential for failure. Either do it or don't do it. You have the power for either. But decide! Do not "try" because you are only fooling yourself that "maybe you'll get lucky." "Trying" is programming absolute failure.

Since human beings can do whatever they put their mind, body, and spirit to, when they say that they will "try," they are lying to themselves and to everybody else. They are expressing their fear of potential failure. And when human beings make a statement out of fear, they are not demonstrating "faith."

Do I mean that you can do nothing? That you are only to sit on your bottom and wait? *No!* Don't "wait." If you "wait" that is what God gives you—the "waiting"—because that is your "expectation."

Worry, the Great "Undoer"

Why do we worry? I think there are several reasons. First, there is the unknown. We worry because we tell ourselves that we don't know what tomorrow will bring. Where will the money come from to pay the rent if we get fired from our jobs? What will happen to ailing Aunt Matilda? Will my child be safe walking to school alone for the first time? We look at the world and we see terrible things that happen to other people and we fear they might happen to us. If we all believed in God, Divine Providence—believed in asking the Almighty and trusting that God will provide our heart's desires—then I doubt that we would fear or worry. So, if we do worry, I suppose that tells us where our level of faith is, or isn't.

Second, I think we worry as a sort of self-motivator. Maybe we feel that, by worrying, we will then start to plan and take action to avoid that which we fear. If we fear for our job, for example, we may then be motivated to invest the time to look for a replacement, just in case. In this sense, maybe worry gives us a sense of security, so we see it as performing a good cause.

But I ask you, where are your efforts and your focus? Improving performance and/or relationships on the current job, or are you mentally breaking confidence with your current employer, leaving him mentally behind you as you look forward to the next opportunity? If we had no fear and trusted in the Great I Am, maybe we would expend our energies to solidify our current job with the expectation, and belief, that all will work out.

The question then becomes: Is worry a "good" thing? The root of worry is *fear,* and that makes fear the motivator. Is it a "good" motivator or a "bad" one? Can we control our destiny? Are we captains of our fate? That brings us back to the concept of cause and effect. If we study well in school, then we *expect* to get a good job, right? In a sense, *expectation* is an expression of *faith,* the opposite of *fear.* We go forward without fear when we *expect* we have taken the action necessary for good things to happen.

But what physical control do we have over whether the *opportunity* will exist just because we have prepared ourselves properly? None. We could do everything "right," and the opportunity may not be there when we need it, isn't that true? Isn't that where the concept of "life isn't fair" comes from? And when we see that life isn't fair, what do we do? Don't we *fear,* and as a result, *worry?*

When negative thoughts enter our head, do they lead to constructive behavior? Can't excessive worry alter our attitude and affect our outcomes? Haven't you seen situations where someone gets so upset with their boss that they worry excessively about losing their job to the point of exploding with the boss and telling him to "take this job and shove it"? We all know what the result of that sort of behavior is going to be, don't we?

That's where the irony comes in. The goal of the person worrying to the point of getting upset is to retain his job, but actually it results in action that causes him to *lose* it. In that sense, yes, we did have control over our destinies, but it's not the sort of outcome we wanted. I think that's where capital punishment comes from. You know, where we rationalize *killing* a killer because he killed. We can only rationalize such conflicting behavior out of fear and a lack of faith in God and each other. Killing the killer gives us a sense of control. But is it? Has killing the killer ever prevented more killing? Don't we reap what we sow? If we live in a society that provides killing as a rationalized acceptable behavior by society then we are creating a society in which killing will be an expected and acceptable response to frustration.

Turn it around. If we created a society in which the appropriate response to killing was to *love* the killer, instead of killing him, realizing that only love can heal the killer's lack of feelings of self-love that causes his unacceptable actions in the first place, wouldn't we then have a society in which everyone learned that *there is no need for fear and that love is the only solution?* Don't we try to do this now? Don't we admonish our children when we see them hitting another child? Don't we try and explain to them that hitting is an unacceptable response to their frustrations?

But, children don't learn what they're *told*, do they? They learn the behavior they *see* in their parents. They learn what behavior is *expected* when they see how their parents deal with their own frustrations. Whenever I see an adult get drunk, or drive wildly on the highway, or strike their child in a store, I immediately think about what sort of home life *they* grew up in and I feel sorry for them and for the parents that demonstrated such behavior to them. But even more importantly, I see how they have been infected with the *fear* their frustrations spawn. I see how "worry" has been ingrained in their lives. Basically, I see how a lack of knowledge and faith in God has left them adrift in the boat of life without a rudder. I see how out of control they feel their lives are. I see the seeds of worry.

I marvel at how I see our society improving. There was a time 20 or 30 years ago when if one saw a parent slap their child across the face in a store, no one stepped in and took any action. It was "socially unacceptable" to interfere with how another parent interacted with their own child, as if the child were a *possession* of theirs rather than the truth, that parents are only caretakers for these little human beings that God entrusted to our care. Today, such behavior is viewed by society as unacceptable, and one can expect another adult to step in and admonish a parent who slaps their child in public. That is a good thing.

Similarly, there was a time not too long ago in America, for example, when whites would look the other way when racial prejudices, or racial slurs, or even racial jokes were demonstrated in public. Today such behavior is socially unacceptable. That is a good thing. They call it "tolerance." But I don't care for that word. To me, it implies that we are just putting up with one another despite our true feelings. I think a better word for it is "love." Love for our fellow human beings. Acceptance of our fellow human beings despite their failings. Only love can heal. Truly, when we see a parent strike a child, we recognize that it is only out of frustration and not knowing how to deal with their frustration. And our hearts go out not just to the child, but to the parent, as well, because we realize that they are lacking a sense of self-love which can only be explained as a lack of understanding of God, because God is *only* love.

God loves us no matter what we do. God accepts us into God's heaven at the end of our mortal lives because there is no place else to go. The Bible tells us that "In the beginning, God created heaven and earth." Period. No other places. Just those two. So, if we're not in one place, we have to be in the other. There is no "hell," no "purgatory," no other place. An all-loving God could not conceive of creating another such place because God accepts all human beings, regardless of what they do, because God knows they didn't mean to perform mean acts. God knows they are just *fearful* simply because of their lack of faith in and understanding of God and God's unrestricted love for all of God's creations.

Take a break and step back from your life for a minute and see Who You Think You Are. Are you a worrier? Do you get frustrated and not know what to do in a given situation? Are you fearful? Can you identify the experiences in your life that caused you to believe you were such a person? Is this how you choose to live your adult life? Do your children frustrate you? Does your boss frustrate you? Does your spouse frustrate you? Are you a "hitter"? Are you a proponent of capital punishment? Are you one of those who condemn the behavior of the Columbine massacre and fail to see the ostracism of the killers from their school society? Do you blame them—the killers—and give no thought as to how the victims alienated them? Is this Who You Choose to Be? Is this how you want to live your life? An eye for an eye? A tooth for a tooth?

As an adult living on planet Earth, you can be anything you choose to be. Could there have been a feudal king had his people not chosen to accept his overlordship? Why did it take thousands of years of oppression before the concept of self-rule and asserting individual rights occurred to the masses? I am reminded of Gandhi, the great leader of India. He brought the all-powerful British Empire to its knees, not by fighting them, but by "peaceful resistance." He simply refused to follow their dictates. He didn't fight them. He explained that he loved them.

He just wasn't going to accept their view of his world. He was going to live his life as *he* wanted to, at any cost. He was incarcerated. He was clubbed. They tried to control him. He allowed them to abuse his body, but not control his mind. He prevailed. The British left and turned the entire country over to him. That is how *he* chose to live his life. Without fear. The one person a bully can't bully is one who does not fear the bully.

These simple truths can be applied to all of life. We can avoid much of the pain experienced in life by simply refusing to see it as *the real* pain. We can simply accept what life doles out, but determine to go forward through life with love in our hearts, and God will see to it that our faith is rewarded. That's not to say that we will eliminate pain, but we will cut it short, and create a heaven on earth for ourselves when we do the right thing by ourselves and by our fellow human travelers through this veil.

Let's go back for a minute to that example of the parent slapping the child in the store back in the 1950s, 1960s, or 1970s. Virtually every adult who viewed such an act felt it in their gut. They knew that what they were seeing was unacceptable behavior. But they did nothing about it. Still, their stomachs were their barometers of truth. Today, many more of them listen to their instincts and take the appropriate action.

But let's be realistic. The appropriate action is *not* to berate the errant parent. That would only be doling out the same negative behavior. Some might quietly admonish the parent explaining to them that that is unacceptable behavior. But you know what? There is an even better way. Ask yourself, if *you* are a child of an All-Loving God's creation and *they* are a child of an all-loving God's creation and *you* know that such behavior is "wrong," then who else knows that too? So, if they know it, instinctively in their own gut, wouldn't it be best to simply *ask* them, "Why are you hitting your child?"

No matter what their response is, couldn't pursuing that line of questioning bring them around to the realization that they *don't* want to be hitting their child? That they don't want to be out of step with society?

Couldn't it raise their own self-perception about how to deal appropriately with their frustrations and how they want to interact with their own, loved, child? Wouldn't this be the loving way to help your fellow human being? If we all lived our lives in this manner, could we help the world avoid another September 11?

Let's look at the root cause again for a moment. Why does a child not yet conditioned by "appropriate behavior" strike another child in their frustration? You know, *before* we teach them that it's wrong to hit another person? Isn't it because their *will* was thwarted? Isn't it because they are not getting what they want? Someone else has interfered with what they want. So they flash hot, and reach out and strike the other out of feelings of frustration at not knowing what to do to get their way. Is that going to achieve what they wanted in the first place?

Say the other child took their toy and they want it back. So, in anger, they strike out at the one who took their toy. And they get their toy back. Mission accomplished. All is well with the world, right? Or, is it likely that the other child will hit back and once again take the toy away. Isn't this the adult world we are living in? Is this how we want it to be? Or is there another way, a better way? We tell our children that to hit another to get their toy back is unacceptable. Then we introduce the concept of "sharing," right? What sort of world would this be if we adults introduced the concept of sharing? Sharing the world's food? Sharing the world's resources? Sharing the world's land masses? Could we eliminate war? Isn't war simply adults "hitting" to take what they want? Is there a better way?

"Therefore, do not be anxious . . . your heavenly Father knows that you need them all . . . and all these things shall be yours, as well," Jesus told us.

What Can We "Do"?

What can we do? Nothing in furtherance of that which we desire. Because desiring it, and thereby taking actions to cause it to happen, *blocks* it from happening. It is as if the act of pursuing a particular outcome acknowledges that other outcomes are possible. But if you can, elevate your consciousness to a level of *knowing* in advance that God will deliver all things desired; as long as they are not expected, then you will get your miracle. Anticipation is like hope: It's a state of not being sure. Doubt enters in and becomes the great undoer. No meddling allowed in God's work!

You can't "do" to get what you want. You can only "be" what you want because you are not a "human doing," you are a "human being." When you do things to get what you want, you are accepting that you do not now have it.

When you accept that you already *have* those miracles you desire in your life, you acknowledge that they are already there in place— whether seen or unseen.

When you declare to the universe that something *is* (meaning it is true), regardless of outward appearances, God has no choice but to give you that which you declare.

Remember earlier in the book, when my father's oncologist declared that my father's death was imminent and I declared that the opposite was true? I declared to that doctor, his staff, and the universe that "My father is now cured." Then I put it out of my mind. No wondering if it could come true. No worrying. Just a quiet acceptance that my declaration was *true* and already a *done deal.*

I didn't have to ask God again, for the very act of asking a second time would be evidence that I didn't believe (know) the first time. If I would look for a particular miraculous outcome, it would never come. The act of looking implies anticipation. When one is looking for something, one is acknowledging that it hasn't happened yet, so it never can. What works is to *know* in your heart that which you want is already a done deal. When it manifests, in the next five minutes or in a year, you won't be surprised. You will be calm and unsurprised, while everybody else around may be jumping in jubilation that it's a miracle.

How can you be instead of do? By *accepting in advance* that your miracle is so, that it has already happened, whether you see any outward evidence of it or not. It is to not be anxious to visibly see the manifestation because you know it is done. This is what God showed me with the three months and three weeks of free meals.

So in the hospital, when the doctor declared my father a walking dead man, I stated *my* truth, "My father is cured!" And he was. We didn't see the evidence of the cure that day, or the next, or the day after that. It was a year to the day that the miracle was reported. As you will remember, I wasn't surprised. It wasn't news to me. I had known it would be for the entire year that it was manifesting.

What If We Can't Wait?

All we can do is believe, and believing is trusting God. Trusting that God will do it, whatever it is we need done and have asked God for in prayer, and knowing that God doesn't need anything from us. Watching isn't a good idea because then we haven't let go. We must let go. That is our job. We say, "Thank You" and then turn our attention to something else. We put the miracle out of our mind.

No one is saying this is easy to do. In fact, it is one of the hardest things to do. It is hard because the desired outcome is important to you. So you have to make it unimportant. If your focus is that God has it in hand, then it is behind you and there is nothing to think about. The matter is settled and resolved in your favor. Just by believing it is.

In times of trouble, I sometimes lose myself and forget these lessons. I worry. I fret. Then I remember. I am supposed to forget about it. I laugh at myself for being so silly as to get all worked up over something I have no control over anyway. I think back to the preceding days, weeks, months, and years that I struggled with a problem, and tried to solve it myself, and I'm ashamed that I lost the faith and forgot the lessons.

The Danger of Caring and Wanting

CARING

Let me put this most dangerous of problems in an example. Let's say you have children whom you love very much. You want nothing but the best for them. You really *care* about them. Because you care so much and want nothing but the best for your children, you might take steps to see if you can't control that outcome. You may try to "direct" your children and their behavior, to help insure that they achieve all that you want them to be.

This "direction" may be expressed as (in your mind) "guidance." But, to your children, it may seem like you are pushing them around, or trying to relive your life through theirs. Worse, while you feel you are motivated by trying to be helpful, what you are really doing is demonstrating that you do not believe your children can make it on their own, or worse yet, demonstrating a lack of faith in your children to do the right thing on their own.

The result of all of this parental guidance is to rob your children of their self-respect, of their belief in themselves. No human being can stand such control for long, and before you know it, they are rebelling against all of your good efforts. They start doing the exact opposite of what you are trying to get them to do.

This only leads to your own frustration, and you try harder to get them to obey you "for their own good." Which, of course, drives them further in the opposite direction. Your frustration turns to anger.

Let's interrupt the story at this point to understand anger. When we get angry, we *think* we are angry with the person who has "caused" our anger. We just can't seem to get them to do things the way *we* want them done. But, the truth is—we are never angry with the other person! We are always only angry with ourselves. We are angry that we can't seem to figure out how to get our way with another person. Not getting our way frustrates us. We *think* our cause is just, our methods fair, our reasons noble. But we just can't seem to get a handle on what to do to achieve our aim. So we get mad. We may even holler at the other person who is not being cooperative. We may even lash out and hit them out of our frustration. But you know what? It is *never* them who make us angry. It is always *us*! We are really mad at ourselves for our inability to get our way.

Aha! So what then *is* the way to achieve our goals? How *can* we get others—like, say, our children in the example above—to do what we know is best for them? That's easy! Just remember that this is the backwards planet.

Caring is the culprit! Caring is the bad guy in this scenario. When we care about something or someone else, we try and force our intentions on it. That act of caring is not a good act. It is a bad act. It demonstrates a lack of faith in the other thing or other human being. As my friend Joe would say, "Think about it." If we expected our children to inherently know right behavior from wrong behavior, we wouldn't feel compelled to direct their behavior, would we? Why don't you believe *in advance* in your own children? After all, they came from good stock, didn't they, being birthed from your own loins?

Ahhhhh . . . maybe you were brought up by parents who expected only the worst from you? And I'll bet they beat you into submission, didn't they?

How *do* children learn right from wrong, good from bad, acceptable behavior from unacceptable? I'll tell you how—they learn by watching their parents, period! If you are an overbearing parent, I *know* your parents were and I can predict where your children will end up on that measurement scale, don't I? They'll bully their own kids, in turn, won't they?

Life is so simple when you realize that everything in life is backwards. Therefore, all we have to do is reverse the process and everything will turn out all right.

Here's the process: (1) Start out *believing in* your children, and always expect that they will do the very best they can. (2) Be an example to your children—*not* the voice of authority. Live your life the very best you can—don't drink so much that you are literally out of your mind, don't get angry and abuse the ones you love, don't get frustrated that things aren't going your way; be patient, and things will go the way you are demonstrating to your children when you don't "care" or try to foist your opinions on them because children do as they *live* (experience), not as they're *told*.

(3) Realize that your children came to earth not knowing anything, so they look to you for an example of how to act, how to behave, how to control frustrations, what to believe in, etc., etc., and they're not going to get it right the first time, or the second, and possibly not even the third time they try out their feelings, emotions, perceptions, etc. After all, they are in a *learning* mode. But the more you *demonstrate* faith, love, belief in God, and belief in them, the quicker they will learn the life skills that will ensure their ultimate success as adults!

The first thing I always told each of my kids was, "I don't care what grades you get in school, just as long as you are trying your best." And, truthfully, I didn't *care* because their grades really weren't important to me. What I was interested in was (a) eliminating the outside pressure on them so that school would be a friendly experience, and (b) letting them know that they were "safe" at home. I knew that the outside world would treat them roughly.

Kids can be mean, teachers can be unfair, employers can be very self-ish. So "home" was their safe haven where they were not going to be "judged." I instinctively knew that if they felt safe and happy and accepted at home, they could take anything the world would dish out. But, conversely, I also knew that if they felt confrontation at home, home could be their least secure-feeling place and really screw them up!

I'm proud that all of my children did well in school and got decent grades, but I still don't care. It's not important to me. However, I take great delight and satisfaction in seeing how well-balanced and well-rounded and loving and kind they are as adults. And, most importantly, how self-confident they are. When my youngest daughter, Penny, calls me to tell me about a big sale she's made, and goes through all of the gory details of how she plotted and strategized to "land the big one," I'm popping my buttons because I knew she could do it all along. She didn't need my help. All she needed was my belief in *her!*

WANTING

Wanting something very badly is the same trap. Sometimes we want something so badly we'll take almost any action to attain it. Imagine a scenario in which someone wants a great deal of money. They may throw caution to the wind to attain it. They might rationalize that they deserve it so much that they have the right to shoot someone and take their money.

We would label such people criminals. Are they a deviant being from another planet dropped mysteriously in our midst? Or humans trying their best to get along in a world that appears to be depriving them? Are they so frustrated and unloved they need to strike out at their fellow humans to get a piece of the action?

Some police officers would advise you to give a robber your wallet and don't resist. Your life may be at stake and you can always replace your wallet and its contents, but you can't replace your life if they shoot you. That's one train of thought. Christ had another to do with nonde-fensive action. Christ counseled that if someone accosted you and demanded your worldly goods, you should give them to them, even the shirt off your back, because if we truly love our fellow man as we love ourselves, we would not want our fellow man to go without. We would *want* to give him the shirt off our back.

The action is the same, but the resultant outcome is entirely differ-ent. The scenario is: The robber demands your money, and you give it to him. But if you give it to him out of *fear*, you *feel* that you've lost some-thing and you truly have. But if you give it over willingly, happy that you're helping your fellow man who is struggling to get along, then you've *gained* something. You've gained peace of mind and a good feeling about Who You Are and What You've Done. For the price of what was in your wallet, you have gained the wisdom of the ages. The same sce-nario occurred, but you are simply defining "good" versus "evil" differ-ently. There is no "right" or "wrong," only our perception of those values.

In Neale Donald Walsch's books, God says that if you want some-thing, that's what God will give you, the experience of wanting. God doesn't give you the thing you think you want: God gives you the expe-rience of wanting it. Why would God do that when God knows how badly we think we want that particular thing? God promises in Mark 11:24 that God will give us *anything* we desire and believe we will get. Think of God as a genie in a lamp who grants all wishes. God has no choice. The answer can never be "No." God has promised that God will give us everything and anything that we believe God will. If that's the case (and this book is in your hands as a testament to the fact that it is), then what's going on here?

What's going on is that God cannot, or will not, countermand *your* decisions about your life.

If you want something, then you must perceive that you don't have it and probably can't find a way to get it. So you determine that you have to get it from God if you're ever going to have it. You ask God for it fervently. But since you don't already *have* it, you think your odds of getting it are slim to nonexistent. Right? After all, God hasn't performed miracles in thousands of years and you are so small and insignificant, why would God waste his time on your petty problems when God has got a whole world of problems to solve for far more important people than you. Besides, if God were going to take care of it, God would have done so already. Right?

Is that the rationale in your mind as you ask God for your miracle? "Oh, please, please, God, deliver my next month's rent to me because I am so destitute and I *want* it so badly. I promise I will be good. I will try and love that old bag next door if you want me to. Oh, I know what a terrible sinner I am and how unworthy I am of Your help, but, please, please, please, give me the money because I want it so much!" Is that how it goes?

God answers that prayer. God gives you what you expect, the wanting of next month's rent.

"Well, how the heck is this miracle thing supposed to work anyway?" you ask. If it is a miracle you are after, how about asking God to put next month's rent in your mailbox? Then you don't take any action or worry about how it's going to get there.

Do nothing? That doesn't make any sense in the practical world, does it? "I can do nothing to advance my desires?" Sure you can. You can (1) ask God in prayer; (2) believe that God does and will answer your prayer; and (3) go about your life and forget your request so you don't start talking yourself and God out of getting it.

That's a tall order, isn't it? That would take a lot of faith. You don't have to have faith, of course. You can go on living your life as if God isn't a part of it. But you won't get the miracle you desire. You can go on trying to take care of yourself, and *wanting* a better life, and not getting it. That's okay. That's how you've been living all of these years. You're used to not getting your heart's desires. You're used to slugging it out in the trenches by yourself. Keep going down that road and you could expend your entire life *worrying* and *struggling* to make ends meet until you are a sour old prune, bitter on life and the world and maybe even hate God for having made your life so miserable.

You can do that. That's the easy way out. But if one of your goals is to figure out how to make it work the way you'd like, what would it hurt to give God a chance?

It is not an easy lesson to learn or enact in your life. But if you can dig inside yourself and find the wellsprings of faith in the Almighty and teach yourself to trust God to the point that you can say "Thank You" *before* you see your miracle, and then leave it alone, walk away from your desire and leave it in God's Hands—guess what? It will drop in your lap.

I can hear your argument already, "Oh, I'm afraid I can't buy into that!" And you couldn't be more true to yourself by saying that because when you say, "I'm afraid," that is exactly right. Fear *is* stopping you from believing in an all-loving, all-giving God. Notice that I didn't say an "all-forgiving" God. I said an "all-giving" God. Read your Bible or your Torah or your Koran a little closer. God does not "forgive" because, from God's perception, we are all God's dear children whom God loves unconditionally. God judges us not, lest we be judgmental. "Unconditional love" means just that. Love that is given without any condition or judgment made.

When I was a boy, I concluded that God must be a figment of mankind's imagination. How could an all-loving God allow the world to be in the mess it is? Inventing a Godlike, all-protecting figure was mankind's way of whistling in the dark to get past the beasts at the cave door. It took me a lifetime and some extraordinary experiences to find out how wrong I was. The truth is, the world is in the shape it's in because we—all of us in our fears—have created it thus. If we want to straighten it out, we're going to have to go Upstairs for help.

We *can* create a heaven for ourselves on Earth. We can do it if we believe we can. The place to start is to start taking care of our fellow man. Be kind to one another. Be especially kind to those who don't appear to deserve it. Feed your fellow man, contribute to their food. We have enough food on planet Earth to feed everybody. We just have a really poor distribution system! Have you enough food to eat today? Have you enough left over to give some to someone who is really hungry? Yes, high-speed Internet would be a nice adjunct to your new computer, but if you have enough to eat, which would be a better expenditure of your excess discretionary money—high-speed modem access or a $2 meal for a hungry child somewhere else in America or overseas?

I have heard it said that if all of the peoples of the Earth could go to bed nightly with a full stomach, we could eliminate war from the planet. Seems like a small thing to do for such a great return on our investment, doesn't it?

As I reflect on the miracles I have received, I note in each instance I let go and let God. When I told the doctor that my father was cured, that was an absolute for me. I never thought about it, or wondered when it would occur. For me, it had already been done because there was no acceptable alternative. I knew my father to be cured at that moment whether any of us could see the proof of the cure or not.

I went about my life and never gave my father's illness another thought. When we took him to the hospital for radiation treatments, I never thought that we were doing anything in furtherance of the miracle. My attitude was even one of humoring the doctors. I never expected that the radiation would have any bearing on my father's cure. We were just going through the motions to help ease his pain and follow doctor's orders. I didn't feel the need to call him up and ask him how he was feeling, or to ask the doctor later to take x-rays to prove that the miracle had taken place. If the doctors had taken the x-rays, I would not have looked at them because they held no information for me. I wouldn't have cared if the cancer was showing up on the x-rays or not. My father was cured . . . and that's all I needed to know. I needed no reassurances.

There have been other times when I wanted something so badly I couldn't let go. My software company was failing. I wanted so much for it to succeed. My home of 27 years was in jeopardy of being foreclosed. I was so close to losing it that I worried about it constantly. Even though I knew how to get miracles, I failed myself. When our miracles don't happen, we tend to see it as God letting us down. But since God is infallible and we see ourselves as fallible, we are the ones not keeping the faith and therefore, we ourselves undo our miracles.

I asked God to save my home from foreclosure. I thought I did it right. The months of making no house payments stretched out into years. The mortgage company went through all the steps to take my house. After they had started the foreclosure process and boosted my interest rate from 8 1/2 percent to 20 percent, and I was struggling to make my normal house payment, they sent me a letter. My credit had been so good before my business started to fail, they had reconsidered and were now offering me a new mortgage at 11 percent. That gave me hope, so I signed the new mortgage documents and sent them off. That looked like the answer to my prayer.

I waited and waited, but the mortgage bills kept coming in at the high rate. I stopped trying to make payments as they were beyond my ability. I began to *worry* about where my new payment structure was. Six months later I received another letter from the mortgage company telling me that they had changed their mind and weren't going to honor the new mortgage. It seemed the idea had come from a progressive vice president in their company; the president had since changed his mind and fired the vice president and was rescinding my new mortgage.

I stopped asking for divine guidance and I took the mortgage company to court to assert my rights and ask the court to enforce my revised contract. The court was unsympathetic and found against me, and ordered me to pay all of the arrears at the higher rate, or be evicted.

I was dumbfounded. I continued to pray, over and over, for my home to be saved from the moneylenders. Then I *looked* to see any signs of my desired miracle. When it wasn't coming to pass, I wondered why it wasn't happening. I didn't realize that I was my own undoing.

Eventually the mortgage lender prevailed and I was evicted. Then I realized something: I was in my home for four years before being evicted. If you were to ask me today what happened to allow me to stay an additional two and one-half years beyond the legal limit, I couldn't tell you, only that God was holding up the process waiting for me to get my faith together. Even so, I failed God and myself.

I was sitting next to my phone wondering what more *I* could *do* to stave off the foreclosure and realized this process couldn't go on forever. I said to God, "I don't know how much longer I can hang on. Surely I must lose the house." As those words escaped my lips, the phone rang and I was told that time was up. I had one week to leave the house or the sheriff would physically remove me.

I bitterly reflected on that outcome for years, still wondering why God had let me down. I imagined there was a bigger lesson of faith that I was to learn by the experience. I was right. After I got time and distance behind me on the experience and the wound had healed, it struck me. God hadn't failed me. I had failed God by not keeping the faith. I believe the lesson for me in that experience was to have an example to share with you to illustrate the "rules" for getting a miracle.

15

The Trick to Getting a Miracle

If there's a trick to getting miracles, here it is: Whenever I try to be logical in trying to make my desires happen, I fail. Whenever I just turn it over to God and let go, and don't be logical, it always comes to pass. Every time we take action, we lose. Every time we don't take action to help ourselves, but turn it over to and trust God, it always happens.

Even though I've been involved in this miracle business for 20 years, and stopped counting my miracles at around number 600, I'm still learning how they work. Recently I experienced a new kind of miracle, what I call the unforeseen miracle. Up until now, my miracles have always been in response to a prayer of thanksgiving made for a particular outcome or need. But God says, "Even before you ask, I will have answered."

My life had become a challenge, again. My software business failed. I lost my home to foreclosure and my car to repossession. I got in debt up to my ears and I didn't know where my next meal was coming from. But I went forward *as if* all would be right. When I lost my home, I took an apartment. Since I didn't have any means of support, I had a friend co-sign. I still had a 17-year-old, beat-up car, and I had faith that God would see me through.

We have this understanding, God and I. I tell God what I need and thank God for it in advance. God knows that the alternatives are: (1) God provides for my existence, or (2) God takes me back home. God knows either one is okay with me. It's God's call. Up to now, God has chosen to keep me alive in my current emanation.

One day, I walked into a car dealership and asked for a commission sales job. They said they didn't need anybody but would take a chance on me. I sold a car every day. That was competitive with the best salesmen in the business. In the beginning, the sales manager said I was the luckiest guy he'd ever seen. After a few weeks, he modified that to I was the best salesman he'd ever seen. One day a customer came on the lot and I approached him. He was a rude, nasty fellow who said he'd been to the dealership before and that he refused to deal with any of our salesmen because they were rude and mean. I asked him to allow me a chance to serve him. He agreed, but he wanted to buy a late-model used car for a ridiculously low sum. I told him I would do my best.

When I returned to the showroom, the sales manager greeted me. "You'll *never* get a sale off that guy," he said. "He's been approached by every salesman we've got. He's a 'looker.' He'll never buy anything." All the salesmen laughed at me.

I worked with that customer for a week. Eventually I talked him down to buying a car older than he wanted, and he came up a little on what he would pay, so we struck a deal. He drove off a "happy camper" in his newer car. "Thank you for being so willing to help me," he said.

That was the day the sales manager stopped telling me I had a lot to learn and asked me what my magic was.

What he didn't know, and what I found difficult to explain to him, was that it wasn't me. It was God working miracles in my life as I had asked. By shifting the responsibility for getting my sales to God, that freed me up to help every customer, and not worry about getting a sale. I had, for example, two customers whose credit was so bad that they should never have been approved for a loan. But God came through and the magic happened for both of them.

Then I got the unforeseen miracle.

I received an e-mail from a distant relative. "God woke me up in the middle of the night with a message for you. He told me I was to send you $5,000, not as a loan, but as a gift. So I'm putting the check in the mail today."

I phoned her and demurred, telling my benefactor I didn't need the money. I told my relative that while it was true I was living from month to month without knowing where my next dollar was coming from, God would provide for me and I'd earn the money I needed somehow. My relative laughed at me and said, "This money isn't from me. It's from God. He gave me the money that I don't need, and then told me to give it to you. He must have some idea in mind what you need it for."

I couldn't argue against logic like that, so I thanked her. I couldn't imagine what God wanted me to do with that largesse. As it happens, soon after I had to leave the job when business dropped in half and there weren't enough customers to make a living from. Thank God for the unforeseen largesse!

To Whom to Pray

Many people—make that Christians—pray to Jesus to get their needs met. Is there anything wrong with that? After all, the miracles come from God, don't they? I believe God does not discriminate by favoring *some* people (Christians) over others. So it is perfectly fine to pray to God through Jesus or in Jesus' name. In fact, Jesus says that all may come to God and ask for God's miracles. "But," Jesus said (I'm paraphrasing him), "if you find that you can't go to God face-to-face because He is too awesome, then feel free to pray to me, and I will take your plea to my Father."

Jesus said, "Whenever two or more are gathered in my name . . ." your miracle request will happen faster and smoother. I have seen this in action. When a group of people come together and ask God for a miracle, it is amazing how smoothly that works. The Realtor story of the dispossessed couple I related earlier is an example. What Jesus meant by "in my name" is that whenever several people concentrate on the same miracle, believing the same way and therefore thanking God in advance for the miraculous outcome they envision, it happens fast and easily. Remember, when we talk about a miracle, we're talking about the "impossible." We're not talking about a consequence of some logical progression of human acts. We're talking about curing cancer or some other impossibility. Impossible, that is, by human logic or effort.

Miracles are God's daily gift to us. It is what God does all day long, for billions of people. It's what God wants to do. It's God's "job." There is no limit to the number of miracles you can ask for. In fact, what God would prefer is that we commune every day, all day long. God wants us to put our faith in God and rely on God to provide for us. God wants us to not do for ourselves, but turn to God for all of our needs. We just can't interfere, and that's where human beings and some faith-based religions get it wrong. They not only seem to want to do it for themselves, but when they turn to God, they want to tell God how to do it. That is their undoing. When you turn it over to God, turn it over. Get out of the way.

It's not easy. If it were, it wouldn't require a miracle. Here is an analogy for how it works:

Let's go back to that earlier image of great danger. Picture yourself steering a bus down a road curving around a mountain. The bus is "you," and the curving road is "your life." Now, in order to be on the right side of God with your life, you must take your hands off the steering wheel and say, "Okay, God, take it!" Then trust that God will steer your bus around the curves. That's illogical, isn't it? You *know* if your hands aren't on the wheel, the bus will go off the side of the mountain, and you will surely crash and die. It would take an enormous amount of faith in God to take your hands off the wheel of your life and allow God to take over and steer around the curves, wouldn't it? That action would defy logic, wouldn't it? Aren't we *supposed* to take responsibility for ourselves? Isn't that what *free will* is all about?

I believe not. Free will, to me, means that we are free to choose a life believing in God or not. The "or not" option spells nothing but trouble for us. Yes, it is not easy to take your hands off the wheel of responsibility for your own life. But are your hands on the wheel doing a good job? I can assure you of this: If you don't believe 100 percent in God don't take your hands off the "wheel" of your life because you will surely go off the "cliff" of troubles. Only those who sincerely believe may be foolhardy enough to take their hands off the wheel for they will know in advance that all will be all right. As Jesus said, "And they shall be called the children of God."

16

God's Choice, or Ours?

When my daughter was paralyzed, she prayed differently from the way I did. She prayed, "Father, whatever you decide about my paralysis is fine with me. You may cure me or not. I trust in You. Thy will be done, on Earth, as it is in heaven. Amen."

I, on the other hand, was going up to God and making specific demands for the healing of my daughter. The difference is, I have come to understand that my daughter was far wiser than I. She believed absolutely in God, and God's love for her. I suspect she *knew* God wouldn't let her down. But she truly meant it when she told God that if it was God's will that she remain paralyzed, she would assume that God had a bigger, better plan for her life than she could see, and she would look forward to fulfilling that plan because she lives her life in service to God.

So how do we reconcile how to pray? If I am telling God what specific miracles to work in my life, is that because of my own inborn fear that maybe God won't do the right thing by me? Uh, oh! Shouldn't I be trusting to God's own wisdom to do the right thing by me?

Here's an example of how I end up telling God what to do, and how limited my vision of what's best for me can be.

The Last $5

The second time my home was threatened by foreclosure and when I was trying to launch a software company, the day I left my old mall manager's job, God delivered a friend who got me a programmer for my product. But the program I needed written was projected to be huge. It could take months or years to write, and there was no assurance it could be written. The program needed the latest in technology, and in those early days of personal computers, we were pushing the limits of what they could do.

My programmer thought it a daunting task but was willing to tackle it on the assumption that the answers would reveal themselves as he went along. I liked his attitude. It spoke volumes about his faith. He told me it would take at least a few months. I wasn't concerned at the time because, even though I was broke, I never considered my money to be my money. No matter how much money I was paid, it was always just enough to pay my bills and provide basic creature comforts. I had rarely been able to save any money to get ahead. I always felt like I was just the go-between from the source of the money and the people who ended up with it.

I had no money to live on. But fortunately, I had been fired from my job at the end of September, and October 1 was the beginning of a new Naval Reserve fiscal year. Reservists are required to perform two weeks of training on active duty every year, so I was now qualified to go again. I sat on my sofa and looked up at the ceiling. "I need a Navy job, Big Guy. Please make one available to me." I said that fully expecting that God had a plan for feeding me until my computer program was written.

Let's step back for a moment. Some might say that I was limiting God in what God could do for me because I was "dictating" that my solution should be a Navy job. They'd be right. I could have just simply said, "Please solve my food problem for the necessary time period until I am earning an income again." God would have done that. But for me, this getting faith thing was an evolving experience. I was, in the words of Indiana Jones, "making it up as I go."

The phone rang. It was a Naval command. They needed a public affairs officer and had been calling around to see if they could recruit anybody on a moment's notice. Most officers have a civilian job, so they can't tell their boss they are taking off without notice. I was the tenth person he had called. He wanted to know if I could go the next day.

This is an unusual scenario. Normally, the commands publish their job openings for Reservists several weeks or months in advance. Then the applicant must fill out an orders request and submit qualification forms; the required waiting time is two months for orders processing. But sometimes when a command is desperate, they can have the two months waived. This was just such a circumstance. I accepted, and was on an airplane the next day.

The good news was the Navy would be housing and feeding me for two weeks, and I would earn enough to take care of my living needs for another two weeks after that. So, a month was miraculously provided for.

Upon my return home, I went through my pay in the next two weeks and found myself back where I had been the month before. The program writing was going slowly. I went back to my ceiling, and said, "Now what? Could you find me another Navy job?" The phone rang again an hour later. It was the Navy with another hurry-up job: Would I accept it? The plane was leaving the next day and I was on it, marveling at my good fortune. The Navy had a rule that a Reservist could only go on one active duty assignment a year, but, if it served the Navy, one could do a second special active duty. Here was mine in record time.

I should have seen the bigger picture at this point, but I didn't. I should have seen that God had planned this for me. God didn't want me to fail and God knew I was counting on God to solve my problem. I should have realized it didn't matter if God gave me food money in monthly or yearly spurts. I should have realized that, since I had turned it over to God, it would come however, whenever.

After I came home again and went through my pay, it was the beginning of December, and I was broke again. On December 5th, I went to the refrigerator to make dinner and discovered that I had no food. I opened my wallet to see how much money I had. Five dollars. I went back to my sofa to ponder this. The programmer called to report he had hit a wall and was stumped as to how to proceed; he did not think his limited skills were up to the task. He said that he had a friend, far more skilled at programming than himself, and was thinking of bringing him into the project. That friend would require an equal piece of the ownership. I agreed to it.

But I thought, "Oh, great, another delay, and I can't even financially hold out until he agrees, let alone last the months that will be required to complete the project." (Can you see how faithless I can be most of the time?)

Sometimes needs can be so pressing, so immediate, that we get scared about the outcome and lose sight of the bigger picture of God's moment-by-moment presence in our lives. As I stared into my wallet at the single $5 bill, I sighed. "Okay, God, I give up," I said. "Looks like I'm not eating tonight, or tomorrow, or maybe ever again. Even if I asked you for a job, it would take a week or two to land it, and then start it, and, then I wouldn't see a payday for at least another two weeks. So, that won't work. Looks like You're going have to find a way to feed me, since I can't, or, if not, I'll die. I'm ready. I'm tired of this constant struggle to keep my home and keep everything going. If you want to feed me, that's fine. If not, that's fine, too." I meant it. I was, finally, just giving up. I wasn't doing it with the thought of "give it up to get it." I was tired. I was dropping the responsibility for my life and turning it over to God.

The thought had barely left my head, in prayer, when the phone rang. It was my former magazine partner, Russ. "Bill, you're not going to believe this. I just got a call from the company we licensed our magazine to. Remember the deal was that they would pay enough cash to settle our last business debts?"

"Yes, I remember," I said half-heartedly, still focused on my resolution to die-by-default of not having any food in the house.

"Do you remember they also committed to paying us royalties when the magazine reached a certain income point?"

"Oh, yeah," I replied. "That was years ago."

"Well, they *hit* it," he declared. "I am holding in my hand a check for you for $5,000. And I'll be sending you a check for $5,000 every month for the next three years!"

I closed my eyes, and said a "Thank You." I could feel tears welling up. I was so ashamed that I had, once again, seemingly lost faith in God and God's miracles, that I had been holding onto my problem and not turning it over to God until the moment before the phone rang. When I hung up, I had a serious conversation with God. I apologized for my failings and fear, for not being able to consistently keep the faith and release responsibility for my problems. I berated myself for having to learn the same lessons of faith over and over again. I thanked God for always coming through at my darkest hours. I promised to never forget again.

I'm sorry to report that I had to sink even lower in my self-misery in the following years and had to keep learning these lessons, repeatedly, and to this day I still cannot count on myself to not backslide.

Here's another example of how I got so mired in my problems that I tended to step in and "help" God.

"I Just Made Commander on the Fourth Time"

When I started my military career 40 years ago, I was an enlisted man. Our commanding officer was a colonel. That rank was so high to me, I couldn't imagine what it would take to get eagles on my shoulders. But I determined that was my goal. I returned to the military through the reserve program while in college. Eventually, I became a lieutenant commander in the Naval Reserve, only two ranks below my lifelong goal. I believed I would make captain, the Navy's equivalent of a colonel.

I was passed over for commander, the next rank up, and a prerequisite for making captain. I couldn't believe it. How could this be? I reflected on my actions. I had the qualifications. In fact, I was one of the best qualified for the promotion. Yet I was not selected. I realized how I had kept control by bringing my file up to date, writing letters, and submitting documents to the selection board. In fact, I had done everything the Navy suggests one do to ensure a favorable review. But still I had failed. I had prayed and asked God to deliver my silver oak leaves as a miracle, but I had not let go of wanting it.

The next year, I decided to do it right. I prayed and asked God for the miracle of my promotion. But as the time neared, I couldn't keep myself from worrying. Surely God wouldn't mind if I participated a little bit, I rationalized. After all, I am required to send in a current photograph. How can God work God's miracle for me if my photo is out of date, I reasoned. As long as I was sending in a photo, it couldn't hurt to add a letter updating my accomplishments, could it? (Can you see the errors of my rationalizing? I didn't.)

I got passed over a second time. Well, that's supposed to be it. Twice is all you get. You can be reviewed again, if you are still eligible, but your file is in the "dead pile."

The next year, I meddled again by writing to the selection board, and I got passed over again. I couldn't believe that God was turning God's back on me. How was I going to make captain, if I couldn't make commander?

The following year, I was still eligible, but it all seemed hopeless. Still, I knew that a miracle is a great, big freebie that happens against logic and impossible odds. I prayed and asked God again. This time, I put it out of my head. I didn't care if my photo was out of date. I didn't care if the board didn't know about my most recent accomplishments. In short, I didn't care. I didn't worry. I decided to put it all behind me and get out of God's way.

I was promoted.

"Wow!" I thought, "I have to remember *this* lesson." I was proud of myself. I didn't think anybody got promoted the fourth time up.

A few months later, I was attending a Navy social gathering of officers. I kept to myself because I didn't know any of them. Standing on the fringe of a group, listening in on the conversation, I heard an officer remark, "I sat on the last commander selection board. I had a funny experience. I was given a file for an officer who had been passed over several times, so naturally I thought he wasn't worth considering. I glanced through it and realized that this officer—somebody named Tucker—was very well qualified, so I asked the president of the board to include it for review."

I walked away smiling. That's how God works. God makes the improbable possible.

I got orders to attend the War College, and while there, I was sitting next to a helicopter pilot, also a commander. I leaned over to him, full of myself, and bragged, "I just made commander on the fourth time up."

He whispered, "Me, too. But it was my seventh time before the board." I was shocked. I asked him how that had come to pass.

"I finally just asked God for it," he said matter-of-factly.

151

Black Tuesday

"Black Tuesday" is the term given to the stock market crash of October 29, 1929, when America was thrown into a panic over stock market losses, and great numbers of companies failed, throwing millions of Americans out of work for years. In our fledgling software company, we faced our own Black Tuesday one day in June.

It had taken many months to develop our software program. Finally, we placed it with a company as a test. Since it was still in its experimental stage, we couldn't charge full price for it, so the income it produced was barely enough for us to scrape by on. We were going broke. The software performed amazingly well. It lived up to our promises to Realtors that it would shorten the turnaround time for selling their buyers from an average of two months to two days. Four thousand real estate customers were processed through the software that year, and *all* bought the computer's selection in an average of a day and a half.

We launched our business, and sold our beta customer a software package at full price. However, that customer wanted some product modifications before taking delivery. The modifications stretched from weeks into months. While the programmers were hard at work, I called on some bankers to offer them the opportunity of marketing the product to their Realtor customers. The bankers hesitated and we got more broke.

When the modifications were done and I went to deliver the product, the customer said they had changed their mind and didn't want to pay that much. Since our price was rock bottom low, and we couldn't go any lower, the deal fell apart. It turned out that customer was also going broke and failed soon afterward.

We had been reprogramming the software for five months and were now destitute. My emotions sank to a low. I was desperate. You would think I'd have learned my miracle lessons by now. After all, I had years of experience with tough circumstances. But, as I've mentioned, it is very hard for me to live in the faith constantly. My thoughts were of God daily, but as a concept, not as a living Being active in my life.

I turned heavenward and asked God to solve our problem and keep us from bankruptcy. For the third time, I was teetering on having my home foreclosed. I thanked God. Then I turned my attention to what I could do to stay busy while God worked. I had gotten a number of real estate companies interested in our software, but none were willing to pay the full amount at once. If we could offer financing, they said they would buy. I decided to arrange for a credit card vendorship while God worked on the larger problem.

I realized that the only bank I had not approached was the one where I banked myself. That's odd, I thought. Why did I overlook the obvious? So I went to my local branch and completed the application for a credit card vendorship. The branch manager invited me into his office. "I'm sorry, Mr. Tucker, but we cannot approve your company for a vendorship."

"Why not?" I protested. It was a hot, sticky day, and I was disheveled, tie askew, sleeves rolled up. I must have looked as desperate as I felt. I was wishing I had taken the time to present myself more professionally.

"Because your company is on the verge of bankruptcy. You are not a good credit risk," he explained.

"But . . . but . . ." I stammered, "it's not *us* who need to pass credit-worthiness. It's our clients who will be charging the money."

"Well, you see, the vendor also has to have good credit. I'm sorry, but those are the rules," he said, apologetically.

As this last hope slipped away, I got up to leave, my shoulders slumping.

"By the way," he said, as an afterthought. "What's that laptop computer you've got with you? Is that your software program in there?"

I replied that it was.

"May I see it?" he asked.

I gave him a demonstration. "Wow! That's terrific," he said. "Have you shown it to our mortgage division?"

I replied that while most of the other large banks in town had seen it, I had overlooked sharing it with his company.

He called someone important at their mortgage division. When he hung up, he asked, "Can you go over there right away? They are very interested in seeing what you have."

The division president met me warmly at the door. I demonstrated the product and he saw the advantage it brought to Realtors and what a great opportunity there was for his company to market it. He said that he would like to enter into negotiations to work out a marketing agreement with us, but cautioned me that we were not allowed to sell any product ourselves or that would kill the deal.

I said, "I'm sorry, then, but I'll have to pass. We are so broke, that I cannot let a day go by without trying to make us money selling."

"How much do you need?" he asked.

"$10,000 a month, just to keep the company alive, with the number of employees we have."

"Done!" he said, and ordered that a check for $10,000 be cut immediately. I walked out of there in wonderment at the check in my hand.

Eventually, the agreement generated close to a million dollars of investment in our company. When we had started the project, we had done so with the agreement and encouragement of the local database owners, the Multiple Listing Service (MLS). When the bank eventually started marketing our product, the Realtors couldn't line up to buy fast enough. Local newspapers and television news shows reported on our success. Sales were going through the roof, and then the roof caved in.

A Sharp Turn Backward Was Required

Our local MLS office began to worry that our product so enhanced their product that our search engine might replace theirs some day. They decided to end their endorsement and access to their data. I protested that they were violating our agreement, but they pointed out that it was a verbal agreement and hard to prove in court.

Once again, our company collapsed overnight. I should have recognized this stumbling block as another opportunity to remain calm and go back upstairs. Once again, we were defeated. We brooded.

"How are You going to get us out of this pickle?" I demanded of God.

The bank called. "Sorry, we're out of this software business. We cannot challenge the MLS," the president said. He had been trying behind the scenes to negotiate a middle ground solution, but had come up empty. MLS was intractable, at least where new home listings for sale were concerned. But they were less intractable when it came to old sold-home data. He had an idea.

"You know," the bank president strategized, "your product could be inverted, and would make an excellent computer appraisal product for valuing homes instantly. The industry is bending over backward to develop something along these lines."

There was the solution. I had been excited from the first at working with this man. Tom was one of the most unselfish, genuinely nice, and faith-based businessmen I had ever met. That was, by now, a requirement we had in our company. We didn't hire anybody or do business with anybody who didn't have a strong faith in God. We felt that we couldn't risk having even one person around who could detract from our getting our miracles. It's illegal to ask someone about their faith in God as a condition of employment, so we didn't do this. It's also improper to bring up religion in any business discussion, so we didn't do that either. But people being what they are, and given the limitations of language in expressing thoughts, it is easy to detect a person's core beliefs.

We went to work to convert our product, envisioning it as a savior for the appraisal industry. We realized that once computers were adapted to that industry, appraisers' employment would be threatened. We knew that our program could be used by them to increase production and lower costs, resulting in keeping them competitive, and in business. The bank, of course, could not continue to underwrite our development costs, but the president went to work to find another sponsoring business. Things began to look up for our product.

The Miracle of Sharing

Some years later, after we converted our software program to a computer residential appraisal program, it turns out appraisers couldn't use it without the approval/acceptance of Freddie Mac or Fannie Mae, the federal government's home loan insurers. These two quasi-federal businesses invited us in to demonstrate and have our product tested along with the dozen other companies that had developed a computer appraisal program. All of the other companies' products failed the test, but ours passed. They asked us how our product worked as efficiently and accurately as it did. We declined to answer on the basis that we did not want to reveal our trade secrets. So they promised to give us the endorsement we needed to sell our product, but they delayed. After four years of waiting, they finally confided that what they had been doing for those ensuing years was trying to copy our efforts and do it for themselves. They finally admitted a couple of years ago that they had failed. They then made overtures about doing business with us, but dragged those discussions out until they fell apart. It seems that they discovered that, once again, our homes were in foreclosure and we were flirting with bankruptcy, so they decided to wait again. One can only surmise what they are waiting for.

To say that all of these evolving events were frustrating would be the understatement of the century. But you know what? We don't *care*. We have given it up to get it or not. Our attitude is that, if these wonderful products are *to be,* then it is up to God to see to it. In the meantime, we're busying ourselves with other things, and not giving a care in the world to that over which we seem to have no control. Neither do my partners and I condemn others for the turn of these events. We strive to *"Judge not, lest we be judged."*

The Clue

I was spending a lot of time puzzling over the turn events had taken in my life, relative to my relationship with God. Why did there seem to be such a roller coaster series of events? Some success, then some backsliding, then success again, then backsliding? Was it to be never-ending? I thought about my actions and my faith, anything that I was contributing to the mix that would cause these ups and downs. It was great that I kept being brought back from the brink of disaster, but why was I on the brink so often? What was I doing wrong?

There seemed to be a message I was missing. Maybe I was too close to the forest of miracles to see the trees of faith. Maybe while I was able to get into a faithful relationship with God when it was necessary, I was not living in the faith all the time. Of course, I thought I was. Not a day passed that I didn't have a conversation with God, seemingly a one-way conversation at that. God had only ever spoken back to me twice.

I had been crushed by the loss of a personal relationship. It took some time for me to realize that I had been overlooking some obvious problems with the relationship. The loss was devastating, and I was angry over it ending. Railing against God and how God could have abandoned me, when I so wanted the relationship to work out, I lashed out against God, driving down the freeway one day. "I want answers!" I demanded. "I know You don't have a voice box, but You can talk to me if You want to. After all, You're God. You can do anything. Please, tell me that I will get through this, and You won't abandon me!" I exhorted. "I want some answers *now!*"

I realized that if God *did* want to talk to me, God could put the words in my head. I didn't have to hear them in my ear. I determined to just drive and leave my mind blank. If I heard a voice, it would be God talking to me. After about a minute, I did hear a voice in my head. It said, "You are only being tested. I'll fix everything."

That's not God! I thought. That's me, making this all up. What an idiot I am. I'm stroking myself. God wouldn't test anybody. God doesn't have to. God loves everybody, regardless of their failings. Besides, I recognize that voice—that's my own inner voice.

I drove on, putting the matter out of my mind. Then I heard a faint voice in the far reaches of the back of my brain and the tone was different. It wasn't the inner voice I was accustomed to hearing. The Voice said, quietly and calmly, "Have I ever let you down?" I got chills. *That* was God. I was ashamed for having questioned God. "No," I answered aloud, "You never have!"

I realized that while God has never let me down, I have frequently let God down. If there is a breakdown in communication between man and God, whose fault do you think it is? I reminded myself.

Eventually, I learned not to care. Not to care about anything I perceived as trouble in my life. Nothing matters, I reasoned, not if it's going to come between me and God. Nothing matters if I am going to get so overwrought that it distorts my view of the world and the people in it. Love is all there is, and my fuming and fussing only interferes with that.

157

The Inside Meaning of a Backward Statement

The statement "You have to give it up to get it" is a backward statement, but a true one. If one doesn't care about the outcome of a particular event, then one doesn't get upset over things not going the way one hopes. Giving it up, you dismiss personal responsibility for a particular outcome. That frees up the responsibility for it and allows God to take control. We do this all the time. Let me give an example.

The Unseen, Unacknowledged Miracles

How do you feel right now as you read this book? Healthy? If you haven't thought about your health today, that is probably because you don't have any current health concerns. Therefore, you are not thinking—worrying—about your health. You are healthy. But could some health problem befall you in the next few minutes? Of course.

Injury or disease can strike without warning at any moment. But the fact you are not worried about it now means you have forgotten to worry about your health and assume good health. Is that not a miracle? The fact that you feel healthy?

We expect to be healthy all the time. So common in our daily experience is this miracle of health that we don't even think about it. We *assume* we will feel healthy today. But if we were aware of God's daily presence in our lives, we could thank God as we arise for providing for our health each day. But it's not worth the effort because the thought that this might not be a healthy day doesn't cross our mind.

It is only when a health issue arises that we become concerned. We may be concerned—worried—enough to seek out a doctor. But on the hundreds, or even thousands, of days that we don't have a health issue, it is out of our mind. On those days, God is performing God's miracle of health for us because we have given it up. Does God require us to thank God each and every day that we have good health? Of course not. God requires nothing of us except faith in God. So when we go about our daily lives assuming good health, we are healthy. Assuming is believing, worry is not.

Ignoring That Which Cannot Be Ignored

Here is another backward statement. Can we ignore that which cannot be ignored? We must develop this skill if we ever hope to receive miracles.

Let's say that you have a problem that is potentially devastating to you. You are so upset about it that you find yourself grinding your teeth and cursing God for allowing it to happen to you. The only solution seems to be to turn to God, and ask God's intercession. You ask God for a miracle solution, and you thank God in advance for providing it. Okay, problem solved.

Or is it? Is it of such great importance that you find yourself waiting, wondering, and worrying about how God could solve this? Can you think of an example where this has occurred in your life? Where you started to unravel your miracle through doubt and fear?

Assuming for the moment that all of us can identify with the above situation, just what are we to do when the issue is so pressing and troubling that we cannot put it out of our mind? Well, obviously, if it is something beyond our perceived ability to control or resolve, meddling in it is not going to serve us. If all we can contribute is worry, that is of no help at all, is it? So we must put it behind us. We must put it out of our head, and busy ourselves with other issues. If we can't help God, we ought to at least get out of the way and let God work. Let us not take responsibility for God.

Assume, for a moment, that God has a plan for everybody. Assume that your life is to fulfill a purpose. If we are constantly praying for things to go the way *we* want them to go, and they aren't, maybe there is a message we're not hearing. Maybe the best miracle prayer we could pray should be not "My will be done" but "*Thy* will be done."

God says, in Walsch's books (paraphrasing), "Pray to Me, knowing that I will fix your problem . . . *or not!*" Either God will provide a miracle or God won't, for whatever reason. Some religions, perplexed as to why God would not answer every prayer (as God promises in Mark 11:22–25), attempt to explain the disappointment by saying, "God answers all prayers, but sometimes the answer is 'No!'"

How could that be? God says (in Mark 11:24), "Therefore, I tell you, *whatever* you ask in prayer, *believe that you have received it*, and it *will* be yours." I don't know about you, but I don't see 'No!' in that passage. I do see a commitment. I see a promise. I see God going on record saying that you and I cannot fail to receive God's beneficence *if we believe*. Once we *ask*, we must put our worries and concerns about the issue behind us and walk away, shrug it off, make it not matter to us any more. Once we ask, we must not ask again. Some people pray for the same thing every day. Why? Because they are fearful that it didn't work the first day. But in the very wise words of President Franklin Delano Roosevelt, "The only thing we have to fear is fear itself." Fear of what? Fear of failure. Fear that there is no God. Fear that the seemingly terrible events in our lives, which we have no power or control over, will defeat us. This is the enemy of our very souls.

Do We Even Need Miracles?

Why do we need miracles? After all, if nothing went wrong in the first place, miracles wouldn't be necessary. The reason God created "evil," like cancer and poverty, etc., in the first place was so God could express Perfect Love for us.

Now, I admit that sounds like backward thinking. In fact, many, many people want to see bad things as having nothing to do with God.

Our world is a relative place. We, for example, cannot know warmth without the existence of cold. Commensurately, how could we know good if there were no evil? How could we know cure if there were no disease? How could we know and experience what love is if there were no fear?

Now, since God is all love, why would All Love create the concept of evil and disease and fear? Isn't the answer obvious? So that Love could conquer all. In other words, God desired to express Love for all of creation, so God had to have a way and a reason to show that expression. If God creates cancer, it is *only* for the purpose of God overcoming the cancer for God's human creation with a miracle in answer to a thankful prayer and as an expression of God's absolute love for God's creation. So, the creation of evil was Love-motivated!

But, you might argue, God doesn't cure *all* cancers in *all* people, so how is *that* an expression of love? To understand this, we have to review how God works miracles.

Let's start from the premise that God loves *all* beings equally. God wouldn't discriminate. That would have to be a denial of God's all-loving nature. So wouldn't God have had to set up a nondiscriminating system for curing cancer? Fortunately, depending upon your view of your world, God did. God created freedom of choice. A human can *choose* to be cured of cancer miraculously, or not. A human has the free-dom of choice to *believe* that God will provide a miracle cure for his can-cer, or not. A human being can choose to believe in God, or in modern medicine operating independently from God. It's a free choice.

What is this freedom of choice we all have? It is the freedom to believe in God, or not. Those who turn to medicine without seeing God as part of that cure are choosing to not believe in a miracle cure. Miracle cures are just too wonderful to believe in, in our "relative world," aren't they? But one can *believe* in the power of medicine and doctors and receive a miracle cure because God gives us what we *believe* in.

So if you don't choose to believe in miracles, I guess you can't have any. And that was your freedom of choice. All freedoms of choice come down to one thing, the freedom to believe in God, or not. To choose to believe in God means choosing Love.

Think about the choices you have made in your life. Have they all been loving choices? Was it your fears that conquered you? And, then, were your choices born out of fear, rather than out of love? God *had* to give us this freedom of choice to be free to choose either love or fear to operate from, or else how could God have a way to express love?

Well, you say, how is that an expression of God's love if God would create a world in which some people could fail to get a miracle? Isn't that discriminatory?

And I would argue, not if you understood the concept. I think it was deliciously depicted in the movie *Bruce Almighty.* In the movie, Bruce has God's powers, and with them goes God's responsibility to help all of mankind answer their miracle requests. Bruce is inundated with thou-sands of requests all day long, and those just from his immediate neigh-borhood.

Think about that for a moment. There are six billion or so people on the planet. All of them are having troubles (or, at least, what they perceive as troubles) all day long, every day. And virtually all of them are turning to God in prayer asking for assistance in curing their troubles. That would really keep God busy. It certainly overwhelms Bruce. So God created a system by which *all* people can invoke their *own* miracle cure-alls. He set up a system on automatic pilot, if you will, whereby *all* people can get *all* the miracles they want just by *believing* that they will. In other words, all people get everything they believe in all day long, every day. This makes *all beliefs* a miracle.

Simply put, what you believe is what you get, and that, by definition, is a miracle. So God answers all miracle requests, all the time, based upon our "freedom of choice." We either choose to *believe* God will cure our cancer and get the miracle of that, or we can choose to believe that God *won't* cure our cancer, and get the "miracle" of that! God gives us nothing but miracles all day long. So it's up to us to define the miracle we choose to get.

Curing Cancer

Recently, a friend of mine in the Naval Reserve sent me an invitation to attend a fund-raiser for her 38-year-old sister, who was dying of incurable cancer. The medical costs just to treat her, without any hope of success, were astronomical. I accepted the invitation, but asked if I could meet with her sister, one-on-one. They both agreed.

Her sister and I sat across a small table and stared into each other's eyes. I asked her, "Do you believe in God?" She looked me square in the eye and said, "Yes. I do." Then I asked her if she believed in miracles, and she answered "Yes" again. Then I asked her if she believed God could cure her cancer, and again she said, "Yes."

Then I put it to her to plumb the depth of her faith. "Do you believe that God will, actually has already, cured your cancer?" Her eyes dropped to the tabletop, and her "Yes" had far less conviction. So I asked her that same question again. And, again, I got the same reaction. So I asked, "Debbie, why do you keep breaking eye contact with me when you answer that question?" It was obvious to me that she was afraid to state unequivocally that she knew God had already answered her miracle prayer request because she had actually come to believe her doctor's prognosis that she was absolutely going to die. He had only given her a month more to live. Had she continued in that belief, I have no doubt that she would really have died by Christmas, the projected date.

I explained to her the process of miracle-getting. I explained how we get exactly what we *believe* we will get. I explained to her that I could not invoke a cure for her. Of course, I could pray for her, but she, like all of us, had her own special one-on-one relationship with God, and God's automatic-pilot-freedom-of-choice-you-get-what-you-believe system is between God and each of us, individually. So it was imperative that *she* believe that God had already sent his cancer-curing miracle to her. I couldn't do that for her. I could only help by raising her perception of what it takes to get a miracle, and pray along with her to strengthen that faith. I asked her to look me in the eye and tell me she actually really believed that God had already sent his miracle cure to her. She did.

Three weeks later the cancer had completely disappeared from her body. And upon discovering that fact, her doctor exclaimed, "It's a *miracle!*"

Are you surprised?

I wasn't.

I expect that you aren't, either.

Seeing?

It has been said so many times, "Seeing is believing," but, of course, that's backward thinking of the sort so common on Earth.

What that implies is, you can't believe it unless you see it. Seeing it is "proof positive." Seeing doesn't require any faith at all. If you can see it, then it must be true, right?

If that concept is wrong to the point of being harmful to mankind, is it because it interferes with man's relationship with God? Then, what would be true?

Turn it around, backward. "Believing is seeing," maybe for the first time. Really seeing, clearly! If one believes first, before seeing, then maybe one can see what one wants to see appear before their very eyes—a miracle. A miracle cure, or a miracle solution, or a miracle assistance with a particular problem will materialize when you first believe in it. Then, and only then, will you finally see it.

17

Reminders for Getting Miracles

The concepts in this book are not unknown to most people, but most of us live in fear and do not see the miracles that happen every day. Many do not yet have the experience of making miracles happen on demand. God has only one job, to demonstrate God's continuous love for us. God is ready to perform all sorts of miracles for us constantly. God is ever vigilant, but I'm sure God feels that we do not turn to God often enough.

Maybe we would be more conscious of our need for a relationship with God if we pinned reminders to our bulletin boards or refrigerators where we could see them regularly. On the following pages I offer a few suggestions for this.

Broken Dreams

As children bring their broken toys
With tears for us to mend.
I brought my broken dreams to God
Because God was my friend.

But instead of leaving God
In peace to work alone,
I hung around and tried to help
With ways which were my own.

At last, I snatched them back and cried,
"How can You be so slow?"
"My child," God said, "What could I do?
You never let them go?"

The Ten Commandments of Faith

1. Thou shalt not worry, for worry is the most unproductive of all human activities.

2. Thou shalt not be fearful, for most of the things we fear never come to pass.

3. Thou shalt not carry grudges, for they are the heaviest of all life's burdens.

4. Thou shalt face each problem as it comes. You can only handle one at a time anyway.

5. Thou shalt not take problems to bed with you, for they make very poor bedfellows.

6. Thou shalt not borrow other people's problems. They can better care for them than you.

7. Thou shalt not try to relive yesterday; for good or ill, it is forever gone. Concentrate on what is happening in your life and be happy now.

8. Thou shalt be a good listener, for only when you listen do you hear ideas different from your own.

9. Thou shalt not become bogged down by frustration, for 90 percent of it is rooted in self-pity, and will only interfere with positive action.

10. Thou shalt count your blessings, never overlooking the small ones, for a lot of small blessings add up to a big one.

God's Letter

Dear Son and Daughter,

Know that I am God. Today, I will be handling all of your problems. Please remember that I do not need your help. If life happens to deliver a situation to you that you cannot handle, do not attempt to resolve it. Kindly put it in the SFGTD (Something For God To Do) box. It will be addressed in My time.

Once the matter is placed into the box, do not hold on to it or remove it. Holding on or removing it will delay the resolution of your problem. If it is a situation that you think you are capable of handling, please consult Me in prayer to be sure that it is the proper resolution.

Because I do not sleep, nor do I slumber, there is no need for you to lose any sleep.

Rest, my child.

Love, your Father

P.S. If you need to contact Me, I am only a prayer away.

Footsteps

One night a man had a dream. He dreamed he was walking along the beach with the Lord. Across the sky flashed scenes from his life. For each scene, he noticed two sets of footprints in the sand; one belonged to him, and the other belonged to the Lord.

When the last scene of his life flashed before him, he looked back at the footprints in the sand. He noticed that many times along the path of his life there was only one set of footprints. He also noticed that it happened at the very lowest and saddest times in his life.

This bothered him and he questioned the Lord about it. "Lord, You said that once I decided to follow You, You would walk with me all the way. But I have noticed that during the most troublesome times in my life, there is only one set of footprints. I don't understand why when I needed You most, You would leave me."

The Lord replied, "My precious, precious child, I love you and would never leave you. During your times of trial and suffering, when you see only one set of footprints, it was then that I carried you."

My God

My God is a God of love.

My God does not discriminate.

My God does not judge.

My God does not find fault with any of God's creations.

My God does not punish.

My God answers all prayers with what the asker believes the answer will be.

My God created all things under heaven and Earth.

My God created the "good" things.

My God created the "bad" things.

My God allows God's children to experience whatever their Will allows them to do. If they do "good," they reap the good benefits. If they do "bad," they, likewise, reap what they sow.

My God allows God's children the choice, and the resultant experience, without judgment.

My God does not side with Hebrews over Canaanites, Crusaders over Ottomans, Americans over Germans, Cowboys over Indians, Christians over Jews, Whites over Blacks, or Blacks over Whites, Jews over Christians, Indians over Cowboys, Germans over Americans, Ottomans over Crusaders, or Canaanites over Hebrews.

My God sides with all of God's children who ask God for God's love and help and believe that God will give it freely, willingly, without reservation just for the asking and believing.

My God gives all of God's children everything they expect; whether they expect "good," in faith or "bad," in fear. God gives them what they expect, what they assume, what they believe.

My God is not a passive God, neither does God abandon God's children.

My God does not create a Satan, but allows mankind to create one in their mind to blame for their own folly.

My God does not create a hell, but allows mankind to live in one of their making, if they so choose.

My God demands nothing of God's children, but God expects faith.

My God gives all.

My God does not know the concept of hate or fear.

My God gives all of God's children everlasting life.

My God would not, will not, and does not deprive any of God's children of everlasting life, no matter what choices they make on Earth.

My God is eternal.

My God made God's children eternal.

My God experiences everything through God's children.

My God is the yin and the yang, the alpha and the omega, the perfection and the imperfection, the beginning and the end.

My God is all.

My God is your God.

My God is everyone's God.

My God is love.

Your God is love.

Our God is love.

God is all there is.

Love is all there is.

My God is real; all the rest is unreal.

Finding God

No life on this Earth finds the real,
deep springs of communion with the Almighty
until it has met adversity and,
by that adversity,
has been forced to a point that it is broken,
utterly helpless before God.

How to Get a Miracle

"Let go, and let God"

"Know that your miracle has already happened"

"FERGEDDABOUDIT"

"Give it up to get it"

How to Pray

"Father, allow me to live the life You have for me."

"Our Will be done."

Believing in advance = knowing

Just say, "Thank You."

What you believe . . .
is what you receive.

The Paradoxical Commandments
By Kent M. Keith

People are illogical, unreasonable, and self-centered.
Love them anyway.

If you do good, people will accuse you of selfish ulterior motives.
Do good anyway.

If you are successful, you will win false friends and true enemies.
Succeed anyway.

The good you do today will be forgotten tomorrow.
Do good anyway.

Honesty and frankness make you vulnerable.
Be honest and frank anyway.

The biggest men and women with the biggest ideas can be shot down
by the smallest men and women with the smallest minds.
Think big anyway.

People favor underdogs but follow only top dogs.
Fight for a few underdogs anyway.

What you spend years building may be destroyed overnight.
Build anyway.

People really need help but may attack you if you do help them.
Help people anyway.

Give the world the best you have and you'll get kicked in the teeth.
Give the world the best you have anyway.

The Box

A man died and went to heaven. He met St. Peter at the Pearly Gates. Upon entering, St. Peter handed him a box.

The man said to St. Peter, "You know, my life on Earth was nothing but a constant struggle. I don't understand why God made life so hard for me."

St. Peter replied, "Then you won't want to look into that box I just gave you."

"Why not?"

"Because it will break your heart. In that box are all of the miracles from God that you could have had, had you but asked."

FEAR NOT,

FOR I AM ALWAYS WITH YOU.

Epilogue

The Miracle of This Book

How does God get our attention when we aren't listening? As we get caught up in our lives and struggle with our problems, fume and fret our way through our daily existence, God *is* here with us, too. God's great heart aches to help us, but our eyes are closed to God; our ears are closed to God. God *wants* to get our attention, but God cannot speak to us directly because it takes our faith to invite God in.

You may recall I started this book with my angry outburst at God over allowing my lovely wife to die.

I railed against God, talking to God directly, vehemently, but God never spoke back. He never uttered a word. Yet, eventually I knew that God was listening sympathetically. Once I opened the door and let God in, God demonstrated God's love for me so consistently and profoundly, that I had no choice but to believe. Then, as I let God into my life and my heart, the miracles kept coming and coming. The miracles I have related in this book are but a sample of the hundreds I have had over the past 20 years. I expect many, many more miracles yet in my life, and I believe that they will come to pass.

As the miracles happened, I promised myself that I would one day share them in a book. I assumed that if the book and its message were worthy, God would find a way to have it published. That you are reading it is the verification that God apparently wanted it written and published. To finish my story, here is how the publishing came about.

I have referred several times to *Conversations with God* by Neale

193

Donald Walsch. One day, I was driving while listening to a National Public Radio interview with Neale Donald Walsch, never having heard of him before. The surprising thing was, I was only traveling five blocks and almost never turn my radio on for such a short trip. But I felt a compulsion to turn on the radio this time. I was electrified by what I heard. Here was a person who had experienced what I had. Here was a person as broken as I had been, and who had turned to *his* ceiling with a similar message to the Great Unseen, who had railed out against *his* God, who demanded answers. And to whom God spoke!

God talked and talked and talked to Neale, every day. God dictated a book to him for publication, promising the intent was to provide God's Word and answers to the problems confronting *all* humans. God dictated two more books to Walsch, and continues to this day to dictate even more. I would be remiss if I took sole credit for this book. All the while I was writing it, it felt as if I was taking dictation myself.

When the radio interview was finished, I had long since arrived at my destination, but was sitting spellbound in my car absorbing every word. I had to get that first book. I thought about whether I could afford it. I only had $75 to my name and no prospect for more. I looked out the window and realized I was staring at a bookstore. "Thy will be done" rushed into my head. I rushed across the street, thinking "God dictating a book, *indeed!* Who does this megalomaniac think he's kidding? I will open the book at random and read a passage ascribed to be 'The Word of God,' and *I* will determine for myself if it could possibly be! *I* won't be fooled by any human protestations of the *Divine*."

I opened the book at random and read a passage. Tears welled up in my eyes. "*Oh my god,*" I thought, "it *is* the word of God!"

As so many no doubt have done, I attempted to contact Neale Donald Walsch. I eventually got through to him, and met him, and shared some of my stories. When he asked me to share some of them in his *Moments of Grace*, I was honored. I was touched when he called me to ask why I had not written my own book yet. I recounted my failed business ventures and said that I was waiting for one of them to come to fruition before turning my attention back to God.

"Has it occurred to you that maybe God doesn't want you trying to work in those areas, but *wants* you to write your book, now?"

The experience helped me remember the second time God spoke to me. Sitting in front of the computer one day, watching a program download, I was brooding over why it was taking so long for our first software program to be written by the programmers. I was overcome by a strange feeling that I should pick up a pen and start writing. I didn't have anything to write, so picking up a pen seemed silly. I tried to ignore the feeling, but it persisted. I thought, this is stupid. Why should I get a pen and paper when I don't have anything to write down?

The feeling continued to persist as an urge within me. I humored myself with the thought: Maybe I'll just write whatever comes to mind, sort of put my questions down on paper and then they might make some sense. Again, the urge overcame me with such force that I started to write the words that rushed into my brain without any comprehension of their meaning.

Questions didn't come to mind, but sentences did, from where, I knew not. I would start to write a sentence, and different words came out on paper from what I thought I was trying to compose. I struggled to change a sentence midway through, but just gave in to the shift in direction my pen was going. I gave up the struggle, and wrote whatever came to mind as God wrote through me in the first person; I wasn't writing the words I wanted to. I felt a burden lift from my shoulders and peace come over me.

This is exactly what "I" wrote, including God's punctuation:

If you turn the choice over to God, why doubt "His" moves?

If you ask for something—are you presuming to tell God how and when to do it?

Either you control, or I control.

Have faith—with faith, all things are yours. Without faith, nothing is.

You can't see it coming, so you doubt. But trust in Me, and everything will come.

Don't *worry* that you don't know how, or why, or when, or who, or by what method . . . or even *if* it will come to pass.

Worry is taking control.

Faith is freedom.

Freedom from the responsibility of your life, and heart's desires.

Anger is not necessary . . . just faith and love.

Just because you can't see it, doesn't mean it won't, or isn't happening.

It—all—*will* happen.

Be patient.

Be busy.

Keep love in your heart.

Trust in Me, and I will do all things.

Be charitable toward your fellow man—understand they don't control their lives either, so they are not responsible for what they do—only for their own faith, or lack of it.

You will be My agent.

You will bring the light of understanding to them.

Forgive the injuries done to you by your fellows—they know not what they do, or even why.

As I use people in your life to deliver My miracles, so, too, do I use others to deliver tribulations.

This is the road to faith.

I love you, My Son. Peace be with you.

About the Author

COMMANDER WILLIAM THOMAS TUCKER, United States Naval Reserve, Ret., was born and has lived most of his life in Milwaukee, Wisconsin, and suburbs. He graduated cum laude from the University of Wisconsin, where he majored in journalism. He spent most of his professional career in public relations, marketing, advertising, sales management, and spent about twenty years as a shopping mall manager. An entrepreneur, he has owned two businesses—a magazine publishing company in California and a software company specializing in real estate software in Milwaukee. In addition, he has taught sales and marketing part-time at a local college. He joined the United States Air Force at 18 in 1960 and retired from the Naval Reserve in 2002 at age 60. Commander Tucker spent all of his adult life in volunteer service to various youth organizations including the Boy Scouts, Junior Achievement, and as a college scholarship chairman of various professional organizations. A widower, he is the father of three children and the grandfather of one.

Hampton Roads Publishing Company
. . . for the evolving human spirit

Hampton Roads Publishing Company
publishes books on a variety of subjects including
metaphysics, health, visionary fiction,
and other related topics.

For a copy of our latest catalog,
call toll-free, 800-766-8009,
or send your name and address to:

Hampton Roads Publishing Company, Inc.
1125 Stoney Ridge Road
Charlottesville, VA 22902
e-mail: hrpc@hrpub.com